Dear Sue

The letters of Bessie Collins from Pretoria during the Anglo-Boer War

Opposite: Elizabeth Henrietta Martyn (Bessie) Collins

Dear Sue

The letters of Bessie Collins from Pretoria during the Anglo-Boer War

Edited by Bridget Theron

PROTEA BOOK HOUSE
PRETORIA
2000

DEAR SUE: The letters of Bessie Collins from Pretoria during the Anglo-Boer War
Edited by Bridget Theron

First edition, first print 2000

Protea Book House
P.O. Box 35110
Menlopark 0102
protea@intekom.co.za

Page design & layout: ANTWORKS Layout & Design, Pretoria
Cover design: HOND BK
Reproduction: Dusk Dimensions, Centurion
Printed and bound by: ABC Press

ISBN 1-919825-17-7

© 2000 Bridget Theron
All rights reserved.
No part of this publication may be reproduced or transmitted,
in any form or by any means, without prior permission from the
publisher and the copyright holders.

CONTENTS

FOREWORD *6*

LIST OF ILLUSTRATIONS *8*

INTRODUCTION *9*

PART 1: '... these awful days of anxious waiting' *21*

PART 2: 'The English are advancing ... Oh! the misery of this suspense' *41*

PART 3: '... Pretoria belongs to England' *55*

SELECT BIBLIOGRAPHY *76*

NOTES *77*

INDEX *103*

Foreword

This fascinating cameo of day-to-day life in Pretoria during the Anglo-Boer War first came to my notice when I was doing research for a MA degree in History in the early 1980s. I used it extensively for information on the period from the outbreak of the war on 11 October 1899 to the British occupation of Pretoria on 5 June 1900, but the diary does in fact cover the full period of the war, ending with the signing of the Vereeniging Peace Agreement in Melrose House in Pretoria on 31 May 1902.

The 95-page letter was written in diary form by Elizabeth Henrietta Martyn (Bessie) Collins and is addressed to her close friend Sue, who lived in Graaff-Reinet. Bessie signs off the letter with the words 'yours faithfully, BC'. From my close association with Bessie's letter over the years I realise that she uses the word 'faithfully' in its fullest sense rather than as the conventional ending of a formal letter. Her diary shows clearly that she was a compassionate, intensely loyal young woman whose sympathies were unquestionably with the Boers. Not only does she provide a lively, coherent and largely accurate account of what was happening in Pretoria in those crucial times, but she also ventures into the more speculative arena of how Pretorians experienced those events. She writes, for example, of the isolation, the inconvenience of curfews, the maddening rumours and the mounting tension. She bemoans the fact that the outnumbered, demoralised Boers refuse to surrender and is highly disillusioned and extremely critical when Kruger and his top officials abandon the town, collect the state funds from the local bank, and move the seat of government to Machadodorp.

BC's letters are of interest not only to historians. They also make wonderful reading for those who are intrigued by the human drama of the civilians who were embroiled in the war in South Africa 100 years ago. They run the entire gamut of the impact of the war on the ordinary people back home: from the huge uncertainty of whether Pretoria would be defended, right down to the inconvenience of being unable to purchase hats and shoes ...

My special thanks to friend and colleague Burridge Spies, a vastly experienced historian and author of *Methods of barbarism?*, the seminal work on the impact of the Anglo-Boer War on civilians in the republics, as well as editor of several notable Anglo-Boer War diaries. He has shown genuine interest in this project and has given most generously of his advice and great academic expertise. Many of the issues explored in the endnotes were debated with him over the coffee mugs in the History Department tearoom at Unisa! Other colleagues, notably Albert Grundlingh, Francois Malan and Greg Cuthbertson were also always happy to provide guidance. Fransjohan Pretorius, as ever, was there if I needed help. My sincere thanks to them all.

I also wish to record my appreciation to the Collins family. When I began to delve into Bessie's background I discovered that she had been part of a very distinguished family who were pioneers in the fledgling republic of the Orange Free State. I also learned that after the war Bessie married her first cousin, William Richard Collins, who features prominently in her letter as 'my dear boy' and who at the time was away fighting with the Boers. He later achieved renown as a member of the Union parliament for many years and, in 1938, as a member of the cabinet.

But then, which was even more exciting, with the kind help of Marie Arnoldi of Ermelo I 'found' two of Bessie's grandchildren: Adv William Richard Collins (Bill) Prinsloo and Elizabeth (Liz) Bakkes, both of whom have their respective grandparents' names! Neither knew that their grandmother had written an Anglo-Boer War diary, so I had the pleasure of showing it to them. Both are very enthusiastic that it has been edited and is to be published. Bill allowed me to make copies of his delightful portrait of grandmother Bessie and let me peruse other family papers and photographs. Liz provided me with the information which solved one of the remaining mysteries about Bessie: why she died at the comparatively early age of 48 years in 1921. I thank them both very much.

It has been a pleasure and a great privilege to edit this diary and there seems no more appropriate time to publish it than at the centenary of the Anglo-Boer War. In the National Archives recently, as I was handling the fragile, discoloured pages rather than my working photocopies, I experienced yet again a sense of excitement and awe: these pages are intensely vibrant and filled with emotions of every conceivable hue.

Bridget Theron
January 2000
History Department, University of South Africa

List of illustrations

Title page: Elizabeth Henrietta Martyn (Bessie) Collins

The house where the Collins family lived	21
George Bourke	22
View of the *Staatsmodelschool* and the school hostel	23
Lieutenant Michael du Toit	25
General RSS Baden-Powell	28
President Paul Kruger	33
General Piet Cronjé surrenders	35
General and Mrs Cronjé	39
RD Collins and his second wife, Carlie	43
Commandant General Piet Joubert	46
Commandant General Louis Botha	51
The looting of the government stores in Pretoria	52
British troops march into Pretoria along Market Street	53
The Union Jack is raised in Pretoria	54
Thomas Voss	56
Lord Roberts	58
Hans Cordua	60
General Christiaan de Wet	62
William Richard Collins in later life	70
WJ Foote, the manager of Payne Bros	71
Lord Kitchener	72
Melrose House where peace was signed on 31 May 1902	74

* The use of photographs from the National Archives, Pretoria, is gratefully acknowledged.

Introduction

Elizabeth Henrietta Martyn (Bessie) Collins was born on 3 February 1873[1] in Bethulie in the southern Orange Free State (OFS), where her father, Richard Dixon Collins (1839–1920),[2] a school master by profession, opened the first school in the dusty little town not far from the Orange (Gariep) River. Richard Dixon and his wife Margaretha Louisa (born Viljoen) had four children, of whom two were girls. Elizabeth, affectionately known as Bessie, was the couple's youngest child.[3]

William Collins senior (1803–1876),[4] Richard Dixon's father, came to South Africa from Yorkshire, England, where he had grown up in a small town called Pocklington near the border of Scotland. After qualifying as a teacher he was offered a post in Cape Town and arrived there in January 1827 at the tender age of 23 years. He later moved north over the Orange River into the Orange River Sovereignty that was under British administration from 1848 to 1854. Collins soon became a respected pioneer in the region and despite being one of the signatories (along with several of his sons, including Richard Dixon) of a petition expressing dismay at the impending British decision to grant independence to the republic of the OFS, he later held several teaching and administrative positions under the Boer government, including that of Registrar of Deeds under President Boshof. When he eventually retired in 1873 the grateful OFS government granted Collins a farm in the Ladybrand district and he called it St Bees after the British town where he had grown up. After his death in 1876 his widow Anna continued to live on the family farm and Bessie mentions in her letter that the wife and children of her elder brother, Willie, 'escaped to our grandmother's farm' during the Anglo-Boer War.[5]

William Collins senior and his wife Anna Wilhelmina (born Whiskin) had a large family of no less than twelve children, two of whom died in infancy.[6] Four of their sons distinguished themselves and became well known in the Boer republics of the Free State and the Transvaal (South African Republic or ZAR). *William Whiskin Collins* (1832–1917), the eldest child, was the author of a work which is now a collectors' item, a book entitled *Free Statia* (Cape Town, Struik reprint 1965, first published in 1907) on the early developmental years of the Orange Free State. William Whiskin became a prominent public figure and was elected to the Volksraad, the legislative assembly of the OFS, in 1862.[7] *Richard Dixon Collins*, Bessie's father, was the third surviving son born to William senior and Anna; he was four years older than the next brother, *John Thomas Collins* (1843–1917). Both John and Richard moved to Pretoria some years before the Anglo-Boer War began. *James Allison Collins,* the youngest son, was Under State Secretary to President Steyn of the OFS during the war and was later appointed registrar of the Appeal Court in Bloemfontein.[8] Bessie refers to him in her diary as 'Uncle Jim'.[9]

The fortunes of the two Pretoria-based Collins families, those of Richard Dixon and John Thomas, will be followed closely because they are so intricately interwoven in Bessie's diary. They come alive against the dramatic backdrop of the war: two English-speaking pro-Boer families who like many other families were struggling to cope with the heartache, tension, frustrations and isolation experienced by civilians in Pretoria while the burghers struggled against overwhelming numerical odds at the front.

In 1879 Richard Dixon Collins and his family moved from Bethulie to Graaff-Reinet in the Cape Colony, where he was the principal of a commercial school for a number of years. It was here that the Collins and Haarhoff families became friendly and little Bessie, who was 9 years old at the time, befriended Susan Elizabeth Haarhoff[10] who was two years her senior. The two girls formed a close, lifelong friendship and Bessie's wartime letter, written some 18 years later, is addressed to Sue.

Richard Dixon Collins and his family were on the move again by 1889, this time to Pretoria where Collins had been asked to take over the principalship of the Ebenhaezer School.[11] Classes were held in an attractive building with bay windows on the south-eastern corner of Schoeman and Van der Walt Streets. The Collins family was given living quarters in the same building and Bessie immediately began to indulge in her passion for gardening: 'I wish you could see how lovely our flowers looked', she writes to Sue. 'We have violets, daisies, marigolds, pinks, carnations and phlox ...'[12]

In 1893 the ZAR government purchased the building and the Ebenhaezer School closed down, but Richard Collins was asked to remain on in a supervisory capacity for the government's new project on the same site – the establishment of a school hostel. The First State Hostel (*Eerste Staatstehuis*), provided accommodation for the boys who attended the State Model School (*Staatsmodelschool*) that adjoined

INTRODUCTION

the hostel and faced westwards to Van der Walt Street. In 1895, Richard's wife Margaretha died.[13] The two eldest children (sons Willie and John) had already left home by this time, but Bessie, her older sister Sophy (Martha Sophia) and their father Richard stayed on in the house. Several years later Richard remarried, this time to Carolina (born Hugo),[14] whom Bessie calls Carlie. The four of them were living in the same 'dear old house in which we have been so happy'[15] when the Anglo-Boer War began.

Richard Dixon's younger brother, John Thomas Collins, and his wife Christina (born Olivier) had meanwhile moved from Bloemfontein to Pretoria in 1879, some 10 years before Richard and his family arrived in the town.[16] John had accepted a civil service post as the chief clerk in the Orphan Master's Department and had bought a family home in Prinsloo Street south, between Schoeman and Skinner Streets.[17] Their older child, a son, William Richard Collins, Bessie's first cousin, is the 'dear boy' in her letter and the man she married in 1903 once peace had been signed. It appears that John and Christina had at least one other child: a daughter called Helen. The two families became very close and Bessie refers fondly to 'auntie and uncle' and describes how they shared family celebrations such as birthdays and christenings.[18]

William Richard Collins (1876–1944) was 3 years younger than his cousin Bessie but their relationship grew close even before the war. With typical Victorian reserve Bessie admits only that William 'was so much to me always'[19] but the two are clearly romantically involved and exchange regular letters, with Bessie fretting constantly about William's safety throughout the war. He was apparently a talented young man who in 1897 used his legal training to secure a clerk's position under JC Smuts, the State Attorney, at the early age of 21. When the burghers were called up at the end of September 1899 and reported for commando service, the 23-year-old William joined the Lydenburg Commando under Commandant PA Dames. To Bessie's chagrin William refused to lay down his arms when the Boers were clearly hopelessly outnumbered and defeated: he was what the Boers called a *bittereinder*, a burgher who would not give up the fight and battled on doggedly right to the bitter end of the war in 1902.[20]

Bessie herself needs no real introduction. She was an educated, well brought up young woman with an English background who was 26 years of age when the war began. In the pages of her letter readers will learn of her fierce pro-Boer sympathies, her indomitable spirit, her great compassion for others, her rather prissy Victorian values, her tendency towards racial prejudice, her love of flowers, enjoyment of reading, fondness of children and her diligent, matter-of-fact outlook on life. In a word, Bessie's candid letter to Sue is not only a graphic 'account of our life during the war' in Pretoria,[21] it is also a window to her soul.

BC's letter to Sue in the National Archives, Pretoria

The 95 page, hand-written letter that Bessie Collins (she signs herself BC) wrote to her friend Sue in 1899–1902 was donated to the National Archives by Sue's younger sister, Miss MR Haarhoff, in 1972, and has been given the accession number A873. Miss Haarhoff's letter is reproduced here in full because it provides some interesting background information on the history of the document and how it came to be donated to the National Archives.

38 Cradock Street
Graaff-Reinet
22 November 1972

Dear Mr Reyneke,[22]

    I am posting under separate cover a further contribution to your Archives.

    These descriptive letters were written by a great friend of my eldest sister (born 1871) from a great friend of hers who signs herself 'BC'. These letters have been cared for by me since my sister's ('Sue') Susan Elizabeth Haarhoff's death in 1951.

    The writer of these letters' closing remarks that she had written in such detail expressing her deep feelings, was because she felt no other eyes would see them but those of my sister. It left me in a quandary all these years – feeling at times I ought to put a match to them and so be loyal to the late BC's wish. But for posterity's sake, I have decided to let the Archives have the care of them. Any bitterness is tempered with much sympathy and sorrow for others. A great lesson in itself.

    The 'William' she mentions became her husband either before or after the war. BC's father came from St Bees, England and opened a commercial school here in Graaff-

Introduction

Reinet for young boys. He was Mr RD Collins and our families became close friends. I was born in 1893 but my birthday book shows Mr Collins was godfather to one of my brothers, Cecil, in 1884.

Mrs Nellie Lucas Meyer[23] hailed from these parts and was truly a stately woman, one who could have graced any court in Europe.

I am the last of our once big family and feel that the fragile state of some of the letters would come to grief by much handling if they were passed round by my nieces and nephews.

Yours truly,
(Miss) MR Haarhoff

BC's wartime letter to Sue is hand-written in a clear, rounded script that is very easy to read. An ink pen is used throughout. The notepaper Bessie uses is of the same kind for the entire letter and is unlined and rather flimsy. The sheets are folded in half so as to provide four writing surfaces for each sheet of notepaper and Bessie writes on each of the four sides. She numbers each new sheet at the top right hand corner. This means in effect that when she starts a new sheet (numbered 2) she is writing on the fifth page. Now (100 years later) the notepaper has become yellowed and the pages are slightly brittle. The edges of the notepaper are also beginning to disintegrate. It is clearly time that a more permanent record of Bessie's memoirs of the Anglo-Boer War be made.

The letter is written in diary form, with dated entries covering the entire Anglo-Boer War period from the outbreak of the war on 11 October 1899 to the signing of peace on 31 May 1902. The first entry is dated 28 December 1899 but is retrospective, describing a number of events which had taken place in the first weeks of the war. The final entry is made on 1 June 1902, the day after the peace agreement had been signed.

The entries were made at irregular intervals and vary a great deal in length. Bessie would write when she had the time, or when there was particular news she wanted to record. There were also times when she was too desperately unhappy to write – notably when there was a major Boer setback on 27 February 1900 with the surrender of Piet Cronjé (for whom she had an inordinate admiration). On 4 March 1900 she wrote: 'We have all been too utterly wretched these last days for me to write ...' and later on the same day: 'Goodbye, I am too wretched to write.'

Most of the entries were made in the year 1900. Bessie made no fewer than 33 entries from January 1900 to the occupation of Pretoria in early June, ending with two very anguished, emotional entries on 4 and 5 June 1900 as Roberts and his troops marched into the town. For the remaining months of 1900 she continued to write very regularly, making 32 entries before the end of the year, providing vivid descriptions of post-occupation Pretoria, heaping scorn on the British soldiers who were teeming in the streets and showing her impatience and contempt for some of the actions of the military government.[24] Nor did her fellow Boers escape her sharp criticism.[25] By 1901 she appeared to have become very disillusioned and despairing about the depths to which the Boer morale had sunk, the guerrilla tactics they were using and the great hardship suffered by their women and children. She made only six rather subdued entries in 1901 and the last time she added to the letter (the only entry in 1902), was on 1 June 1902.

The letter is highly readable because it is so frank, unaffected and so full of human interest. As the daughter of a school master, Bessie was well-educated and expresses herself clearly, but some of her spelling and punctuation tends to be erratic, which has made certain minor editorial adjustments necessary.

Editorial policy

BC's original letter is not subdivided except into dated entries, but because the Anglo-Boer War fell into three distinct phases (see below) for the people of Pretoria, it was decided to present the published version in three separate parts, each headed by the relevant historical landmarks, dates and an appropriate quotation from Bessie's diary. Explanatory notes have been added at the end of each section to identify the people named, provide details on various battles and, in some cases, to give historical perspective to what Bessie wrote. As far as possible the text remains exactly as BC penned it, because it is felt that the charm of the diary lies to a large degree in its candour. However, the following editorial changes were considered necessary:

- BC's tendency to **abbreviate** the dates of many entries has been standardised by completing the date in full but with the added

INTRODUCTION

details in square brackets. Thus if BC wrote 16 Dec it now reads 16 Dec[ember 1900]. The same policy has been followed in the case, for example, of K[roonstad] although OFS and even OF State have been left as Bessie wrote them.

- **Spelling** errors have been corrected in most cases and there are quite a number of these. Among other things, Bessie used lager instead of laager; scarse instead of scarce; escapt instead of escaped; baloons instead of balloons; kneif instead of knife; cappie instead of kappie and sowing instead of sewing. She also spelt many names incorrectly, notably Smuds (Smuts), Van Reen (Van Reenen), Baden-Powel (Powell) and Hofmeyer (Hofmeyr). In cases such as these the spelling has either been corrected, or in some instances an explanatory note has been provided.
- **Capitalisation** was very popular at the time Bessie wrote her diary. Recently I learnt that using the upper case is again becoming more fashionable than it was five years ago, so I have tried not to be too heavy-handed with Bessie's capitals. Her consistent use of the lower case for *boer* has been retained.
- The **grammar** has not been changed except where there was some doubt about what was meant. Bessie wrote well and very few changes have been necessary.
- **Punctuation:** Where the content of a particular entry deals with a number of different topics and Bessie (to save paper, perhaps?) wrote one continuous piece, the text has been broken up appropriately into paragraphs (without tampering with the order of the text). Commas have been added where necessary, but Bessie's exclamation marks (often followed by a word beginning with a lower case letter) have not been altered because they are very characteristic of her writing style. Ach! how I wish ... and Oh! why can they not ... have thus been left unchanged.
- **Weights and measures, time and currency** have been left as Bessie wrote them. Note that 1 pound (lb) is 0,455 kilogram (kg). To avoid confusion, the time 10 [am] or 10h00 has been inserted where necessary to explain 10 o'clock, for example. Reference to the currency used in the Transvaal at the time, that is, £.s.d., has been retained. Note that £1 was worth R2 in 1961, but this is no longer realistically the case.

Setting BC's diary in its historical background

A great deal has been written on the Anglo-Boer War of 1899 to 1902 – perhaps more than on any other event in South African history.[26] There is now no doubt that all the people of South Africa, not only the two rival armies, were touched by this war and that its impact was profound. The emphasis in recent works has to some extent swung away from the military strategies employed in the war and indeed from its political aspects, and has turned instead to what Smuts calls 'the human experience' behind the war, 'the vast tragedy in the life of a people'.[27] BC's diary fits well into this category because it is intensely human; it is her own personal account of how she experienced the war as a white woman in Pretoria, the republican capital. Her diary sees the Anglo-Boer War primarily as a social phenomenon, but it should not be read in a vacuum; it is necessary to put her personal experiences into a wider historical perspective.

Historians have debated the causes of the war almost *ad nauseam* and have shifted their interpretations and reinterpretations over the years. An early theory that Britain started the war to redress the grievances of the Uitlanders, the foreigners in the ZAR, has since been discarded and the emphasis is now usually placed on British imperialism and expansionism. It is argued that Britian was determined to maintain her hegemony in the region in the face of competition from other countries such as Germany. The aggressive political and economic ambitions of important role players such as Alfred Milner, the British High Commissioner in South Africa, Joseph Chamberlain, the Secretary of State for the Colonies, and the stubborn obstructionism of President Paul Kruger have also variously been placed under scrutiny in a search for the roots of the war.

The discovery of minerals in South Africa in the second half of the 19th century, diamonds at Kimberley in 1867 and gold on the Witwatersrand in 1886, is of course central to any discussion on why the Anglo-Boer War was waged. It has also been suggested that the mine magnates played an important part in causing the war. In order to take control of the gold mining industry and maximise their profits by manipulating the all-important black labour supply, the mine owners wanted to remove Kruger's inefficient government and assume political (in collaboration with British officials such as Milner) and economic control of the ZAR. This could only be done by force of arms because 'Oom Paul' in Pretoria refused to be cowed by the might of imperial Britain.

Introduction

Whatever view one takes on what caused the war, it is clear that many factors played a role. BC's own opinion, expressed in her characteristically forthright manner, is that the war was 'unjust' and that a greedy Britain had 'dealt shamefully and cruelly with us'[28] in order to take the land and the mineral riches away from the Boers. She writes:

> We have sacrificed thousands of our best and bravest men and now all is in vain and the country they love so dearly will be wrenched from them by those hateful English who have no peace unless they can have the best of everything. The cruel heartless tyrants. Can people be surprised at the bitterness when you think of a mighty nation crushing a pitiful handful of boers for the sake of their gold? ... they meant war all the time ... we are crushed and they will have the land and come and gloat over us ...[29]

Although Bessie's view is simplistic and understandably over-emotional, it is probably not very far from the truth.

When the war began on 11 October 1899 the British were confident that by Christmas 1899, a mere three months later, the war would be safely over.[30] The Boers apparently also thought that the war would be brief.[31] Certainly neither side anticipated that almost 32 months would elapse before peace was eventually signed, or that it would prove to be 'the costliest (over £200 million) and the most humiliating war that Britain fought between 1815 and 1914.'[32]

The course of the Anglo-Boer War can be conveniently divided into three stages. In the initial stage, the bulk of the British troops had not yet arrived in South Africa and this gave the Boers the opportunity to launch successful offensives into Natal (where they besieged the town of Ladysmith) and on the western front, where they laid siege to the British garrisons at Kimberley and Mafeking. The commandos also succeeded in inflicting a number of significant defeats on the British forces during so-called 'Black Week' in December 1899.

In retaliation the British poured more troops into the country under a new Commander-in-Chief, Lord Roberts, and the second phase of the war began. Roberts reversed the Boer ascendancy, systematically relieved the besieged towns and took Bloemfontein on 13 March 1900. He then began a relentless march north into the Boer republics, occupying all the main towns on his way. After taking Johannesburg on 31 May he entered Pretoria on 5 June 1900. The war appeared to be over. The British leaders were jubilant and Boer morale hit an all-time low. Smuts writes in his memoirs: 'The fall of Pretoria ... [was] ... a turning point in the history of the war.' The Boers were demoralised, it had been a case of 'everlasting retreat, retreat – wearying, dispiriting retreat. At every stage of the retreat the Boer cause became more hopeless, the Boer army smaller in numbers, and the Boer resources more exhausted.'[33]

But despite all predictions, the Boers did not surrender and the war entered its third and final phase. The Boers abandoned conventional warfare and launched into guerrilla warfare epitomised in the daring exploits of Christiaan de Wet and the able leadership of the young Commandant General, Louis Botha. Small mobile units made lightning attacks on the British forces and rode off before they could be captured. They dogged the cumbersome British lines, destroyed their communications and seized their supplies. This time the British answer was to resort to what has been called a 'scorched earth' policy. Boer farmsteads were burned and all stock destroyed, which meant that the burghers had no support base. Homeless Boer women and children from these farms were taken to makeshift concentration camps, usually in desolate outlying districts. The concentration camps were part of a military strategy, designed to put pressure on the Boers to surrender, and were not intended as places of shelter. The appalling conditions in these camps led to a massive death toll of about 28 000. The scorched earth policy also left African people without any means of supporting themselves and they too were carted off to camps. The total number of deaths among Africans in these separate concentration camps is still largely unknown but was probably in excess of 14 000.[34]

When the three-pronged British strategy of scorched earth tactics, concentration camps and driving the Boers against lines of blockhouses and barbed wire was intensified by Kitchener (who had taken over as Commander-in-Chief from Roberts on 29 November 1900), the Boer fortunes waned still further and it became clear that the struggle was hopeless. In May 1902 Boer delegates met at Vereeniging to decide whether they should enter into peace talks with the British. The outcome, late on the evening of 31 May 1902, was the signing of the Peace Treaty of Vereeniging in Melrose House in Pretoria.

Because BC's letter is written from Pretoria and her experiences are not of the entire theatre of the war, her diary is divided into sections which differ slightly from the conventional pattern discussed above. The first part of the diary covers the period from the beginning of the war in October 1899 to the occupation of Bloemfontein on 13 March

1900. Bessie describes Pretoria's reaction to the early Boer victories and then the dreadful setbacks, culminating (for Bessie, at least) in the surrender of Piet Cronjé at Paardeberg on 27 February 1900.

The second part begins in March 1900 as Roberts, after a period of comparative inactivity, eventually begins his advance along the railway line towards the north. This was particularly significant for the civilians in Pretoria and they waited in restless anticipation, not knowing what their fate would be. They had no idea whether Pretoria would be defended or not. They were kept in absolute ignorance, and this nearly drove Bessie to distraction. She found the suspense absolutely crippling. 'It is so hard to sit here day after day and wait for them to march in' she wrote on 15 March 1900, and again, 'the Government keeps everything so quiet'[35] ... 'our hearts are heavy, we fear the worst'[36] ... 'we just live a day at a time and never know what will become of us ... You can imagine how troubled we all are. The Government will not let out anything. We only know the enemy is coming'.[37] The suspense builds up until Roberts enters the town on 5 June 1900.

Part three is summarised neatly by Bessie: 'Pretoria belongs to England.'[38] The republican 'holy of holies' was in British hands and both Boer republics were annexed to the British crown. The Transvaal Colony was put under military government and Bessie passed a great deal of comment, much of it critical, on how this administration was run. In 1901 her entries became far less frequent and she despaired of the war ever ending. She was sickened by the stories of the suffering in the camps and the death and destruction of the war. On 1 June 1902 she wrote, almost in disbelief: 'At last, at last, we have Peace', and even the most conscientious of editors could not possibly remove the capital P from her Peace!

The historical value of the diary

The value of this document lies in the insight it provides into a wide variety of aspects of civilian life in the republic for the entire duration of the war. Bessie is well informed and intelligent and she is certainly not reticent in expressing her opinion. She sheds new light on a number of issues including the Red Cross activities in Pretoria; the antagonism of the Boer people in Pretoria towards the Hollanders; the prevailing attitude towards the African people in Pretoria during the war; the growing feeling of isolation in the town and the shortages the families had to suffer. From the diary we also learn that the women at home were critical of the wanton looting committed by the burghers at the front. We read of the efforts of Pretoria's women to make clothes for the burghers at the front, and about the 'lying' newspapers, the heartache of loss, and the tremendous blow to those back home when Cronjé surrendered at Paardeberg. We also gain new insight into how disillusioned and cheated some of the civilians of Pretoria felt when Kruger and the top officials left Pretoria for the eastern Transvaal, taking the state funds with them.

There is fresh insight into the post-occupation period in Pretoria, the dissatisfaction of the local people who had to submit to British rule and the efforts of the authorities to clear the town of women who were likely to 'cause trouble'. The execution of Hans Cordua, on 24 August 1900, an incident shrouded in mystery and not without controversy, is also discussed in some detail. BC expresses her 'disgust' and dismay at 'the way our women carry on with these Khakies'. She even goes as far as to criticise Annie Botha, the wife of the Commandant General: 'She always has a lot of officers about her. It does show such bad taste to say the least.'[39] This is information that has not received any previous attention. But perhaps most important of all, BC's diary gives us insight into the 'ordinary' day-to-day hardships of the war, the deprivation, the tension and the grinding isolation suffered by the civilians in Pretoria.

Insight into issues such as these and the general credibility of the diary are enhanced by the fact that recent research into Bessie's background and her life after the war have revealed that she was part of a prestigious family and that, like many of her forebears, she had a keen sense of public responsibility. After her marriage to her cousin William Richard Collins on 21 October 1903, they moved to Ermelo where William practised as an attorney in the firm Louw & Collins. In 1916, by which time the couple had four children, William was elected as a member of parliament, and in 1938 he entered the cabinet as Minister of Agriculture and Forestry, a position he held until his death in 1944.[40]

Bessie died when she was only 48 years old.[41] She had always been a compassionate, public-spirited woman: this is certainly evident in her diary. During the Spanish flu epidemic that swept the country like wildfire in late 1918, killing thousands of South Africans, she volunteered her services as a nurse. She did not regain her strength after surviving the initial onslaught of the virus and died on 4 October 1921.[42]

'... these awful days of anxious waiting'

Pretoria from within, October 1899 to 13 March 1900. From the beginning of the war to the occupation of Bloemfontein.

Pretoria
28 December 1899

Dear Sue

I have thought so much of you and all our other friends in the Colony that I must write although I do not know when you will get this letter, if ever. Oh! child, it is dreadful to be cut off from the rest of the great busy world like this. We do not even know if all our friends are alive. We have lived through years and years of sorrow and deep anxiety during these two months. It will soon be three [months] since Martial Law was declared.[1] It seems ages since we have closed school[2] and everything has been turned upside down.

Our house has been turned into a Red Cross Hospital.[3] We have the front part and the garden to ourselves. The linen room has been changed into a kitchen for us because we did not care to be too mixed

The house where the Collins family lived. This photograph was taken in the 1950s just before the building was demolished.

up with the Red Cross people. They gave us a tiny stove and I do the cooking. We are only four[4] so I do not find it very hard work. Only the miserable little stove gets so dreadfully hot that I sometimes feel as if I would like to hang through the window. It is so pleasant to be such a small family: from 76 to four is a difference, and no mistake. If it were not for this war we would be quite happy.

This section of the Red Cross belongs to Mr Bourke.[5] He is a small energetic little man who has a great deal to say for himself and everybody else. He has not had much education but is always ready to give his opinion on any subject. There are 8 nurses besides the matron[6] who is a tall, strong, red faced woman. She was matron in the new hospital in Bremersdorp[7] and had to leave when the war broke out. She says everything was in such nice order and she had a hundred chickens coming. It must have been hard to leave it all. Fancy, she knew General Buller's[8] sister. She was a teacher in Cape Town. He is a man of 60 but is very strong. I am supposed to be a Red Cross nurse too but as there are never many patients here I have done no nursing yet.

We have 89 officers imprisoned in the Model School[9] which is on our ground. We had some of the class rooms fitted up with beds for our wounded in case we had not enough room here. Well, one afternoon we received orders to clear out the hospital things and to hand the school over as a prison for 50 officers. Sophy and Carlie[10] went over to fold all the sheets when they [the British officers] came. They at once began to speak to them. They all admired the building so much and wanted to know when the school had been closed and how many boys we had. Then they said they were so hungry and asked father to get them their supper. He of course would not do so without orders from the landdrost.[11] But as it was getting late he said father might do so and he would pay him for it the next day. We made a huge urn of coffee and sent them a dozen tins of sardines, 6 tins of golden syrup, 4 lbs of butter and 40 lbs of bread. Father went over to see if it was alright and found them seated round our dining room tables, which had been commandeered, and they were so grateful to him. They said it was quite a feast!

[The] Government has certainly done all they could to make them comfortable. They have fitted up a kitchen, bathrooms and the yard is lit up with electric light.[12]

George Bourke

PART 1: '... these awful days of anxious waiting'

View of the Staatsmodelschool *and the school hostel*

They get books and newspapers, [and] are allowed to buy what they wish and I can tell you Sue, they don't believe in stinting themselves in any way. The day they came they looked so dirty and untidy in their khaki suits[13] but the next day [they] all had new suits and slippers. They order all sorts of things to the value of £25 a day. Still, it must be an awful life. The younger men play games in the afternoon. They have about 12 soldiers who cook and do their washing. We had three of them laid up here in the hospital. They once said to father [that] they did not believe a word the papers said about our victories but now I daresay they have to believe, as their numbers have been increased from 50 to 89 besides almost 3000 soldiers.[14] It is late, so I will say good night.

Friday 29 [December 1899] Dear Sue, it is such an age since I had a chat with you and so much has happened that I find it difficult to know what to tell you first. After Martial Law was proclaimed, all our boys[15] of course left. It was during the September holiday so there were only about 20 with us. Almost all our boys are at the front as more than half of them were 16 years of age and over and as you know, they are burghers at that age and so must give their services in time of war.[16]

We do not even know how many of them are still alive. They are scattered all over the two states.[17] So far we have heard of two who have gone. The first died near Mafeking of fever, Pretorius.[18] He was a monitor. A splendid young fellow, 21 years of age. The best boy we ever had. Just before the war he passed his 3rd class Teachers' Exam so well. It was such a shock to us to hear of his death. We had a broken-hearted letter from his father a few weeks ago. He was ill for 11 days and suffered much. He sent beautiful messages home and said they must not mourn for him, he was ready to go. It was so hard that none of his people were with him.

The other was one of our old boys, Coetzee. His father was also killed. A few of our boys have been wounded. I wonder if we will ever have this home [re]opened for them, and how many we will see again after the war? Oh! how everything has been changed. Johannes van der Merwe,[19] the teacher who boarded with us, has gone to Mafeking. We are expecting him here on a short visit. We are all very fond of him. He is such a fine character.

William[20] is at Ladysmith. He was home for six days a few weeks ago. He came quite unexpectedly and I actually did not know him! He had a beard and it changed his whole face! You know our men do not shave so they all sport beards. William was not at all well when he left for the front, but he came home so well and splendidly strong. Dear old boy, if only he comes safe out of this hateful war. I receive a letter from him almost every day. He says the heat and the flies are unbearable at Ladysmith. When they have their meals it is a regular fight to see who will get the most [food], they or the flies. They are all getting so tired of waiting for Ladysmith to surrender.[21] I wonder how much longer General White can hold out.[22] So many of his men have been killed by our shells and many more have died from fever and other causes. There is not much hope of the enemy getting through to reinforce them, as our men have all the best positions.

None of us will ever forget the first fight our men had at Dundee.[23] We got the news on Sunday and oh! Sue, the misery we endured that day. We at the same time received news of our dreadful defeat at Elandslaagte.[24] It makes my heart ache even yet, just to think of it. I will tell you about Dundee as I heard it from Lieut du Toit,[25] Miss du Toit's (who visited GR[26]) brother. He was wounded badly in the leg by a shell and is in town. He says the men had been on the march the whole night and they were dead beat and faint for want of food when they got on the hills overlooking Dundee. They had only three guns

PART 1: '... these awful days of anxious waiting'

with them and expected to have a 6 hours' rest and food before beginning the attack. When all of a sudden the general gave the word to fire. He says they were all so stunned by the order because the guns were neither cleaned or protected and the enemy had 18 guns! Just at first he felt too paralysed to do anything. He says it was awful. There was a perfect rain of shot and shell and the noise was of course deafening. It is a marvel any of our men came out of that awful fire alive.

He told us of some wonderful escapes. One boer[27] was firing from behind an ant heap so he said to him it was a dangerous place. At last he again said: "Get up, if a shell comes it will take you away ant heap and all.' The man changed his place just in time. A moment later, a shell burst there and the ant heap was gone! He saw a boy of 12 years of age fighting bravely until he fell! Is it not dreadful that such a young boy was allowed on the field? [28] He says in spite of all the awful sights he saw during the battle he could not help laughing. Once he saw an old man with a long white beard who had got a great fright, run like a hare and he cleared stones and bushes as if he was a young boy of 18 instead of an old man.

Lieutenant Michael du Toit

Lieut du Toit was wounded early in the battle but his men got so discouraged when he fell so he would not let them carry him off the field and said: 'Do not let them take our cannon except over our dead bodies!' Of course this he did not tell us. He is very modest. He was so sure of defeat that after he was wounded he wrote in his notebook: 'Just had an engagement, all lost. Love to Katie' – his wife. He [then] fainted and one of his friends carried him off the field. He says he does not know how they got out alive because shells and bullets simply rained over them. Once a shell burst close to them and his friend fell with him.

After it was all over and Dundee was taken, all the wounded had to be laid in one large operating room and he says in spite of the agony he suffered he could not help laughing. Some of the men were so ridiculous. The doctor took a bullet out which had gone almost right through one man's body. It was still quite smooth. He was so disgusted because he said who on earth would believe that bullet had really been in his body. Another man's bullet had become very long and he was so proud of it and asked how much a jeweller would charge to make a brooch of it for his wife. Lieut du Toit saw one man who received a bullet through his head take it out of his mouth and coolly going [go] on fighting after he had put it in his pocket! His [Mike du Toit's] wound was so bad that he sent for his wife and Miss du Toit to come and nurse him. But I will tell you the rest tomorrow. Good night.

Sunday 31 [December 1899] I said I would tell you Miss du Toit's impressions of Dundee. Well they were of course dreadfully unhappy about Mike, because before they left someone told them that he had seen Mike and his foot had been amputated! It was such a shock to them. They found him very weak and suffering much pain, but were thankful that his foot had been saved. He was in the hospital with several officers. Miss du Toit and Katie lived in a cottage close to it. This cottage was just as the people left it when they fled. She says she saw the looting[29] going on and it was awful. The men, mostly the low class of men from Johannesburg,[30] went into those deserted homes, took what they wished, [and] smashed beautiful furniture, even pianos and fine paintings. She saw lovely baby dresses and women's clothing and shoes lying about. In some houses they turned open the canned fruit and left it to spoil. I can't understand their doing such things. The fruit they could have used for their sick. They [also] broke open jewellers shops and robbed as much as they wished. Some wore jewels in their hats to the value of £10 or £20! Is it not wicked that our men soiled their hands by doing such wicked things? We felt so sad about it and still we have been blessed so wonderfully, in spite of all our many sins and shortcomings.

Miss du Toit also visited the English camp and picked up several little things which she showed us. One was a little Bible, [there was] also an egg-cup, some notepaper with the Hussar's stamp [and] a little sewing case with needles, cotton and darning cotton, which belonged to a soldier. She also picked up several letters. One from a girl to her lover. In it she says: 'When you are victorious I shall say that you and you alone have gained the victory and annihilated the boers!' She also visited the wounded soldiers and did little things for them. Fancy, they were attended by their own people and only got bread and butter and tea three times a day. Mike was so sorry for them that he got Miss du Toit to take them eggs and milk. As soon as Mike could be moved, they came [home] to Pretoria. They are still anxious about his foot. The shell is still in it. One doctor took 46 bones out of it. They are thinking of having an operation.

After Dundee came that defeat for us at Elandslaagte.[31] Oh! Sue it was so awful. So many we knew lost their lives there. Some people declare that the Germans and Hollanders[32] were drunk. You may have heard that a patrol was sent ahead of the force. They captured a train with liquor and instead of destroying it as they were ordered to do, they all drank as much as they wanted and filled their flasks. So when the English hemmed them in they were many of them helpless.[33] It was a horrible slaughter. When those horrible lancers came, they just butchered the poor creatures. I don't know if you remember Mrs Minnaar[34] – her eldest son was killed there, and I don't know how many Hollanders and Germans.

Here is a little story one Hollander told Rev Bosman.[35] He was lying next to an old boer during the battle and was terribly frightened. When the old man saw how he was trembling he said: 'My brother, I see you are frightened, let us pray.' So there, amidst the awful hail of shot and shell and the roar and rush of battle, the old man calmly knelt and lifted his voice in prayer until all his fears left him and in that hour of his bitter need he, who never prayed for himself, learnt the power of prayer.

After Elandslaagte followed the other great battles, of which I daresay you [have] heard. We have had wonderful victories and comparatively few lives lost on our side, but Oh! child, our hearts ache for the broken-hearted women far away in their English homes who are weeping for loved ones, gone forever. We long and pray unspeakably for peace but we feel very hopeless some times. It almost seems as if that happy time will never come. The English seem quite ready to carry this unjust war to the bitter end in spite of the awful loss of life on their side. If they cared as much about 20 men killed as we do about 1 man's life on our side, they will cease this needless slaughter.

Now, Sue dear, before I go on I want to wish you all that will be best for you and yours during this New Century.[36] Child, is it not a solemn thought that before its close you and I will have crossed beyond the mystery of the veil and beyond all the sorrow and troubles of this life! We are living in very dark days. Our hearts are so often heavy with care, if not for ourselves alone but for all those of our friends as well, who have had such heavy loss during these last months. But surely our people will come out of all these trials as gold tried by fire.

How I long to see you or to hear from you, but that I suppose is impossible. I wonder when you will be able to read this letter?[37]

3 January 1900 Mr vd Merwe came on Saturday and is still with us. He has told us such interesting tales about his life in laager.[38] He is at Mafeking and they are all getting pretty tired of waiting for Baden-Powell to surrender.[39] The boers agree that he is very smart. He is also fond of a joke, it appears. He generally sends a despatch with the white flag after a shower. Our men were at first so eager to hear what it was, because they hoped that he was going to surrender, but in the meantime he sent all the women and children out for an airing. The report is always about some trifle but those poor women enjoy the air.[40] Our men say they all live in cellars under Mafeking – what a weary time they must be having. William arrived here this morning. He does look so queer with his beard. He got leave for a week.

General RSS Baden-Powell

I must tell you about Dingaan's Day.[41] It is, as you know, the great national day in Transvaal. We had [a] service in our church.[42] The congregation was almost as large as on Sundays. It was so pleasant to see the bright hopeful expressions on almost all the faces, because the evening before we had received news of our victory at Colenso.[43] After the opening service Mr Bosman asked us to stand while he read the telegram which Oom Paul[44] had received. It was an impressive moment when that large congregation stood so silent with hearts full of deep gratitude, listening to the grand news of victory. The language in which the telegram was worded was so beautiful. It began with these words: 'The God of our fathers has again given us a great victory over our enemies.' We thought the way in which they referred to the prisoners [was] so dignified: 'We have also captured 150 of their best men, the flower of their army, who charged us so often and so gallantly.' The whole service was very impressive and I am sure we all felt better for having been there. Surely our people will never forget this Dingaan's Day. We only had 30 men killed and wounded.[45] Although we were so grateful for our victory, our hearts ached for the broken hearted women far away in England, who would weep for loved ones lost forever. Oh! Sue child, my heart bleeds for them and I would gladly give all I possess if I could comfort them.

When, oh when, will this horrible war cease? We are weary to our souls of all the misery and bloodshed. I cannot understand how the English can calmly see their own men annihilated like this and [yet] continue this hateful war. One man who went over the battlefield at Colenso says it was too horrible. The whole country[side] was heaped with dead and wounded. Some were calling for their mothers and wives, others were crying to God. Some poor fellows were gazing at the photos of their friends, or holding their letters in their dying hands. It is stated that the English loss was 5000 killed and wounded.[46] Days after, many of the bodies were still unburied and the vultures fed on them. Some people believe that Buller was wounded at Colenso[47] and others say that he is a prisoner in our school!

4 January [1900] It was a lovely afternoon so Sophia and I went out calling on our bicycles. Since Martial Law was declared we are not allowed to ride out of town or be out later than 6.30 [pm][48] which is a nuisance because that is the best time to be out, as it is so hot. We heard at Mrs Voss'[49] that 60 of our men [were] captured and 16 were killed.[50] And we can so ill afford to lose any at all.

Saturday 6 January [1900] We have just returned from our weekly evening prayer meeting. Today we were made happy by good news from the front. Our people have taken an important position at Ladysmith and it is almost impossible for Gen White to hold out much longer.[51] We will be thankful when that place is taken, because then our men can move faster.[52] Ach, how weary we are of this miserable war. We also heard that at Colesberg the enemy have been beaten back.[53] How I wish they would settle this business now. But it appears they mean to fight to the end as they have voted more money to get new guns and more men are coming. William wants us to go and eat ice cream with him, so I will say good night.

Sunday 7 [January 1900] It is such a hot close day, I do hope we will get rain. We have had a good deal of fruit this season. We had early rains too. We expect a fine crop of yellow peaches and apples, even grapes a little later. During this week we have been busy gardening as are many others, because if this war lasts much longer we will need all we can get out of our gardens. I induced Sophia to take a share because I am sure it will be good for her health. After some trouble William managed to get me some flower seeds.

You have no idea what a weariness to the soul shopping is these days. One day we spent almost 2 hours in buying a few little things like cotton lace and so on. I do not know what we will do later. Hats and shoes are running very low. Sugar and milk equally so. When the war began it was said we could at least hold out for a year, but I doubt it. There has been so much wicked waste of all sorts. Now at Dundee. Our men would go into a store, and one would cut open a bag of sugar and another would come and say 'There is poison in that bag, cut open another', and so on until there were a number of bags cut open and the sugar wasted. Whole tins of biscuits were tumbled out into the streets. Oh! it makes me so sad that our people, at least some of them, do such things, because it seems so mean after all the help we have received. Another thing which grieves me is that some of them steal so dreadfully. They will steal anything from a horse to a knife or a plate.[54] It is very sad. Of course it is not the majority who do these things, I am thankful to say.

Today the *Volksstem*[55] published a special [edition]. Our people have taken a number of the forts at Ladysmith and some more cannon, but 15 of our men were killed and we do not know how many were wounded. It is so dreadful for us to hear of the loss on our side and yet we ought not to expect to gain victory without loss.

The rain is coming down grandly. Sophy, William and I returned from our walk just in time. I don't think I told you about our Christmas this year. Well, it was a very, very sad day in many homes where there were vacant chairs and loved ones gone forever. The town was very quiet. We all thought of friends and relatives away in the different laagers and of brighter Christmas Days in the past. It was not at all like Christmas Day and we could not wish one another a merry Christmas but gave our wishes for a happier one next time. Although some say the war won't be over even then. How are we to live through all the weary months if that is true?

After Colenso several [British] officers were again sent to the school.[56] There are almost a hundred here without those who were again taken during this week. One, Colonel Hunt, was wounded in both legs and was sent to our hospital.[57] He was in command when the 10 cannon were taken. He was so terribly cut up about it that he was raving mad for a few days. When they found him on the field he had a paper pinned on his breast with the words: 'This is the man who lost the 10 cannon'. He would not allow the doctor to take it off. When he was here the first day he often moaned 'Oh! they smashed us up terribly!' Poor man, we felt so sorry for him. He would not stay in the hospital longer than three days. On Christmas Day he sent the three nurses each a lovely silver napkin ring with their name and the date. Was that not kind of him?

I suppose you have heard all about that young scamp Churchill's escaping.[58] If he had waited until the next day he would have been released, because the General[59] sent a telegram granting him his freedom. He is a tall, dark, handsome young fellow and has escaped four times.

21 January 1900 Dear Sue, what a long time it seems since I wrote to you. I was interrupted so often while William was here because the silly boy always had to go for a walk, a ride, or we had to talk to him. He left last week. It was hard to see him walk off looking so strong and brave and to think that we would perhaps never see him again. Oh! this weary, weary time of anxious waiting and heartbreak. Sometimes it seems to me God's curse is on us and we will never 'win through'. How the English are pouring in![60] Is there no end to them? We are such a pitiful little handful and our poor men must be getting so weary of it all. Last week a few more of our men were buried here. So many of the best known men are lying in the graveyard. Yesterday one was buried again. We saw him a few weeks ago. He looked so well and strong as if death could not touch him and now he is gone and leaves a wife and baby girl. Oh! child, every precious life we have to give makes the thought of having to lose the country a thousandfold harder.

This week we got seven patients. One is a Du Plessis. He is dying and his poor little wife is sitting there with him in the ward, waiting for the end. He was very bad during the night and prayed: 'Oh! my God, help me now or I die.' He was wounded in his stomach.

We have heard so many reports of Buller's death that we almost believed them, but yesterday we heard that he had been wounded through the mouth at Colenso and lost almost all his teeth. That is rather hard lines as he has only one eye.[61] Oh! Sue child, we have just heard that our people are fighting at Colenso. The English attacked them yesterday and today they are still fighting.[62] To think that we were having such a calm, quiet, restful day and our poor men were facing death in all its most hideous forms. So far four have been killed and 10 wounded. We never realised how beautiful peace was until now and how we long and pray for it.

On page 5 somewhere[63] I told you of some cannon and fire positions our men took at Ladysmith. Well, we lost all 74 of our men killed and almost 100 wounded. It was awful. We could hardly believe it. We could never quite get at the truth of the matter but it appears they stormed the place and then there was some miserable mismanagement[64] or something and we had this awful loss. It was worse than that [at] Elandslaagte. Now we dread every engagement and are almost afraid to see the lists of wounded and dead.

My brother Willie[65] has been commandeered to do special police duty. Lottie says in her last letter that they send him all over the country and she is so afraid that the English will capture him. He had his Christmas dinner in our Piet Cronjé's tent. He is one of our best and bravest generals.[66] At the beginning of the war they spread a report [that] he was killed. I shall never forget – our hearts died within us, and how thankful we were when we heard he was alive.

30 January [1900] This month is already at an end and still there is no gleam of light and we may have to drag on for God only knows how many weary months. Child, none of you will ever know the sorrow of these dreadful months. Surely a curse will rest on all those wicked men who caused this unjust war. I am bitterly disappointed in the English. We have always been taught to admire the English as the bravest and most upright and generous nation on earth but they have dealt shamefully and cruelly with us. It will be many a long year before the ill feeling and hatred will die out of the hearts of the people.[67]

Sophy and I came home on Saturday after a pleasant visit with our friend Mrs Wood. She is a sister to Joe Pott. I don't know whether you remember him. He was wounded at Ladysmith on the night when the English destroyed some of our guns. Four of our best known young men were killed that night. Joe says he fell when he was shot through his lung but was conscious when a soldier came up and stabbed him in his side. He told him it was a mean thing to stab a man who was down. This brute said with a laugh: 'Oh! you are a d … boer!' Poor Joe, he had an awful time and suffered such agonies [that] he prayed [for] them to put an end to him. He is in the Girls' School Hospital.[68] We went to see him. He is getting on but it will be a year before he will be able to go about his work.

The greater part of the last 5 days our men have been fighting at [the] Tugela [River] to prevent the enemy from getting to Ladysmith.[69] It was a terrible fight. But we have again been wonderfully blessed and they have been repulsed with fearful loss. I am afraid to give you the number of their [the British] killed because it is so large I am in doubt as to its correctness, but it is very far over 1000. Oh! the poor creatures who are sent to their death by thousands and what for? We rejoiced, but our hearts were heavy for our brave men who were killed and can so ill be spared. Five were buried here. One, a Mr Jan Malherbe[70], who we knew well, leaves a wife and child. Another, Charlie Jeppe[71] [was] his widowed mother's only son and [her] sole support. About 67 of our men were killed and 220 wounded.[72] We feel it a heavy loss but it is little considering that they fought for five days[73] against such terrible odds. One of our boys was killed there on Wednesday. He [had] only fought for two hours when a bullet went through his brain. His father lost a leg in the First War of Independence[74] and now he [has] had to give his son.

We heard from Rev A Hofmeyr,[75] who is a prisoner in the school and came to the hospital as a patient (dysentery) that Katie Murray has been divorced from her husband. Poor girl, how she must have suffered. Sue, I wonder if you long for news from me as much as I do from you. It is miserable not even to know whether all our friends are alive. But it is no use grumbling. Goodnight.

26 February [1900] Dear Sue, it is actually more than a month since I last wrote. But so much has happened and we have had such anxious days, full of dread and sorrow, that somehow the time went without our taking note of it. Child! we are beginning to dread the result of this unequal war more every day. We have lost some of our best men. General Cronjé is surrounded by 30 000 English.[76] Kimberley is relieved[77] and that wretched Rhodes[78] is once more free to go and make more trouble for us. Oh! how the wicked seem to flourish. Yesterday Pretoria was gloomy about the news from our brave old General Cronjé.

President Paul Kruger

In our church[79] in the evening Rev Bosman read a message from Oom Paul asking us to pray for him and all our burghers with him. He had sent a telegram asking the nation for their prayers as he was surrounded and saw no way out unless God helped. There was dead silence and one could feel the congregation was deeply moved. We had a short service, then a prayer meeting. Things are very dark and if God does not help we are lost and oh! the bitterness of the thought that after all we have had to endure, we must lose all. We can't endure the thought and the nation is crying to heaven for help with one voice. We had another prayer meeting this evening. Tomorrow is Amajuba Day[80] and we pray that once again the nation [will] be blessed with a mighty deliverance. Our men have been fighting hard at Tugela for the past week. Two of our boys have been killed again and some wounded. We hear the most awful stories of how the English treat their dead and wounded. Today I saw some horrible photos of English soldiers lying unburied 10 days after the fighting at Tugela. It is late, so good night.

27 February [1900], Amajuba Day This morning there was great excitement in our yard amongst the police and Mr Opperman and Dr Gunning[81] – the latter two men manage the affairs of the officers who are imprisoned in the school, and by and bye we heard that 3 of them had again escaped.[82] We cannot understand how they managed seeing they are guarded by 12 men day and night. We fear that there are traitors amongst us. I hope they will be captured.

We are all anxiously waiting for news from the front. Sophy and I went to service this morning. There was a large congregation and everybody looked very much depressed. It is a dull cloudy day and things look miserable all round. I have just heard how the officers managed to escape. They turned a knife into a saw and cut an opening into the ceiling board and then they cut the electric wire at eight o'clock last night. All the lights went out and during the confusion which followed, they cleared. They chose their time well. It was a dark windy night. They must have taken days to get the knife ready and to cut the ceiling. There were ladders in the gymnastic room, which they used to get at the ceiling.

This has certainly been a very gloomy Amajuba Day. Perhaps it will be the last one in the history of the country. We all say God forbid! But what have we done to deserve otherwise? We are heartsore and weary and all is so dark. Poor Oom Paul, how trying these days

PART 1: '... these awful days of anxious waiting'

must be for him. He receives telegrams up to 11 o'clock at night sometimes.

1 March [1900] Another day of suspense. Oh! the misery of it all. We hear no news except that our poor men are still fighting hard at Colenso and that Gen Cronjé is still surrounded. He lost 40 men and 60 wounded. How we dread to hear that some of our boys have been killed. Brave old Piet Cronjé! How we will rejoice when he is free once more. Surely our prayers for him will be answered. These dreadful English, how they are still pouring in. Oom Paul left for Ladysmith last night. We do not know what his mission is. We received several patients from Colenso this afternoon. Four [are] badly wounded. We heard that all the Natal hospitals are to be cleared of our patients. That means that our people expect to retreat. It will be better, because then the two states can guard our own borders and leave what does not belong to them. What do we want with more land, let us keep what we have. We are expecting to hear things which will surprise many of us within the next few days. This has been a dull rainy day. We have heard no more about the escaped officers.

We have about 4000 prisoners at Waterval[83] now. I am dreadfully troubled about them because if ever their people surround us they will be beyond control and if those rough soldiers break loose on Pretoria, I dare not think what the result will be. Maybe we too will see English shells fly[ing] into our lovely town and destroying everything. It is impossible that we will be left in undisturbed peace for long. Here everything is so calm and quiet. People go about their work, one would not know that only in the next state, two nations are killing each other. The awful horror of it all! Two nations worshipping the same God [and yet] shooting each other like dogs. And there seems no chance of

General Piet Cronjé surrenders at Paardeberg on 27 February 1900

its coming to an end soon. We got in some provisions, but not clothing. I do not know what our poor men will do if the war lasts through winter. Shoes are very scarce.

4 March [1900] Dear Sue, we have all been too utterly wretched these last days for me to write. Oh! now I understand what David meant when he said: 'All thy waves and billows have gone over me.' We could get no news, only those horrible rumours flying round from no one knows where. But on Friday it all came out. Our poor brave old General Cronjé with about 2000 of our men were taken by the English, and that on Amajuba Day.[84] The bitterness of it all! We could not and would not believe it. It seems as if God Himself has forsaken us and cursed us because our poor men were entrenched in the river, it appears, and the rain caused it to come down amid the awful fire of our enemies. It breaks my heart to think how they must have suffered. And here we were all in church praying for them. We cannot understand and can but cling to Him, our only support in this heavy darkness. He only knows what Transvaal and OF State people are living through in these awful days of anxious waiting.

We hear nothing. Hundreds of women do not know where their relatives are, or whether they are still alive. Ladysmith was relieved on Wednesday[85] and we only heard officially on Friday. We heard that there was heavy fighting and the Pretoria laager [commando] was cut to pieces – you can imagine how the mothers, wives and sisters feel. William was on Lombard's Kop[86] guarding the cannon and we have no idea what has become of him. About nine o'clock last night we had a telegram from Mr vd Merwe. This is what he said: 'Thank God, still alive!' from Van Reen's Pass.[87] So they must have retreated from [the] Tugela [River area] where for days and days they had been fighting against overwhelming odds. We dare not think how they must have suffered and how worn out and dead tired they must be.

Now no one knows what we will hear next. To us it appears there is no hope. We have sacrificed thousands of our best and bravest men and now all is in vain and the country they love so dearly will be wrenched from them by those hateful English who have no peace unless they can have the best of everything. The cruel heartless tyrants. Can people be surprised at the bitterness here when you think of a mighty nation crushing a pitiful handful of boers for the sake of their gold? Now they fling it in our faces that we declared the war. If we had not done so they would have overwhelmed us at the start, as they meant war all the time and

PART 1: '... these awful days of anxious waiting' 37

only waited to get all the troops out. Oh! what is the use of writing about it, we are crushed and they will have the land and come and gloat over us. If only Piet Cronjé was not in their hands. What an awful humiliation it is. To think of them rushing to the Cape Town station to stare at him and jeer at our brave old general. It makes my blood boil to think of it. How will he bear it? Why, oh why, have we to drink of this cup of shame? Goodbye, I am too wretched to write.

After supper: We did not go to church today as it was so rainy and we cannot afford to spoil more things. Last night we came home drenched from our weekly prayer meeting. The streets were like rivers. It is wonderful how soon [often?] and how unexpectedly it rains floods in this country.

Auntie and uncle[88] were here this afternoon – of course we talked 'war' all the time. We heard a report that our dear old Cronjé has been rescued from the English.[89] We do not know if it is true but if it is, how we will thank God for it. What joy there will be over the whole land. Then our men will fight with fresh courage! If it proves a false report ... Ach!, I will not give such a miserable possibility a thought.

[On] Friday morning, while I was getting breakfast ready, Carlie came in and said: 'Guess who is here?' To my surprise I found it was one of our dear boys[90] about whom we had been so anxious as he had been with Cronjé when he wrote to us last. His name is JJ Booyens. We all called him 'Oupa'[91] because he is such a queer old chap but we are very fond of him all the same. He had been home for two weeks and was so bright and hopeful about things. He was sure we were mistaken. Cronjé was alright and things were going on well. About 5 o'clock [pm] we heard all the bad news I told you of. It was sad to see how crushed Oupa was. My heart ached for him. He has five brothers with Cronjé and does not know if they are alive.

He told us a great deal about his life on commando. They have had a very hard time. He was in that fight at Magersfontein[92] and says he saw the most awful sights. Those lyddite shells are the most horrible things. They spoil the food our men carry into battle in their bags, so that they can't eat it as it becomes bitter. So for hours they must fight and get faint for want of food. They also make the men quite heavy and numb so that for a time they are helpless.[93] Then those balloons are another thing which give a lot of trouble, because they find out where our horses are and then the enemy can place shells right amongst them. They also sometimes use dum-dum bullets. They are certainly an invention of the devil. They expand when they come in contact with muscles or bones and explode and crush the latter beyond cure.[94] Oh! those English, how will they answer for all they make us suffer. We can easily change our Mauser bullets into dum-dums but our Government had strictly forbidden it.

I suppose you will be surprised to hear that I still attend to my garden but one must work or we could not live through [the] days. On Saturday I sowed some seeds. I do not think I told you that Nelly Burger (Mrs General Meyer[95]) was our neighbour for almost a year. She has grown so old-looking and worn and I am afraid she is not at all happy. I don't see how she can be with a man so much older than herself. He is one of our generals but we hear all sorts of yarns about his being a coward. Poor Nelly, what a blighted life hers seems. Child! how I wish I could have a peep at you tonight. I long for news from you all. I wonder how my little Chicken and dear Gerty are?[96]

Monday 5 March [1900] Sophia and I went to sewing class this afternoon. I do not think I told you we have sewing classes every afternoon from 3 to 5.30 [pm] to make clothes for our men at the front.[97] [The] Government supplies all the things. We only go three afternoons in the week. The women were all very quiet this afternoon and we heard no news. It is a shame we are kept in suspense like this. As to those detestable newspapers, they ought all to be sent to the North Pole! They are just crammed with lies. I am sick to death of the whole business. Poor old Cronjé is eating his heart out on board ship in Table Bay. We are done for... I wish we were all dead! Oh these English – how I hate them. Good night... what is the use of writing. I will let you know when they come and smash us up here. I wish they would look sharp [because] this suspense drives one wild. Oh! our poor, poor burghers, to think it was all in vain!

Wednesday 7 [March 1900] No news from William yet. This suspense is dreadful. The people are becoming so discontented because [the] Government keeps back all the news. We would all a thousand times rather know the worst, than be kept in ignorance. Oom Paul left for Bloemfontein and we hope that they will come to terms somehow. Surely there has been enough bloodshed on both sides.

Oh! these rumours! we hear all sorts of dreadful things. Someone spread a report that 1700 of our men [who] are at Jacobsdal [are] wounded and thousands have been killed but we get no official notice and no lists of killed or wounded.[98] How the women who had relatives with Cronjé stand it, I do not know. Do you know that he fired the first shot of the last war of independence and again this time, he began the first fight.⁹⁹ I wonder how his poor old wife feels? She was with him in the laager but he sent her home a little while ago. Every Sunday morning those two used to walk to church hand in hand!

Yesterday three of the officers were released because they are so disabled that their fighting days are over forever. The one was an only child of very rich people. His left arm is paralysed and his face is a little disfigured. Poor boy, how shocked his mother will be when she sees him.

One of our cousins was killed last week.¹⁰⁰ He was the eldest son, such a fine young fellow. He was shot dead next [to] his brother. The Frames¹⁰¹ have had a great sorrow. Their youngest brother Norman was commandeered to guard the prisoners at Waterval and shot himself by accident. It was an awful shock to them. They were getting a box of food ready to send to him. The fowl was still in the oven when the news came. It is one of the saddest of the many sad things which have happened during this dreadful war. They were stunned and could not realise that he was really dead. Just a few days before they received a bright merry letter from him. They are wonderfully brave people. It made one's heart ache to see how bravely they tried to bear their sorrow.

General and Mrs Cronjé

8 March [1900] It is a rainy afternoon and as I have nothing to do, I will have a chat with you. How lovely it would be if I had you here instead of having to write. I wonder, oh, I wonder, when I will see you again, or have the pleasure of receiving a letter from you? Yesterday afternoon I was made happy by a letter from William. Poor boy, he says they had an awful time. He and some 40 men had to cover the retreat of the rest of our men.¹⁰² The enemy fired on them and the bullets came so thick and fast that it is a wonder they were not all killed. Only one man was slightly wounded. They slept in the veld in pouring rain with hardly any food. He was sick and had an attack of dysentery so badly [that] he could hardly get on. When he did manage to find a doctor, he had no medicines with him. At last one of the men recommended muddy water, of which there was a good supply. He took it three times and it cured him. You have no idea what a hard time our poor men have had. I wonder they are not all quite heartbroken.

Tuesday 13 [March 1900] We heard that Bloemfontein has been taken.[103] We are so anxious about our brother Willie and his family. Of course we cannot communicate with them now. It seems hard that the English should be allowed to have things all their own way. Those poor Free State people! I am so sorry they even joined with us. It would have been better if they had not cast their lot in with this unhappy country. They always went on so peacefully and quietly and now they have to lose all on our account. What a pity we can't die of broken hearts like people in novels! Father was quite sick when he heard about Bloemfontein. Now I wish they would hurry and finish all. When they have crushed us, I wonder if they will feel very proud of themselves? Still, it is some little comfort to us to know that they had to call out their reserves and could only crush us by overwhelming us by their thousands. They have had to pay a heavy price for their victory, but I suppose they will make us bend very low to make up for all the humiliation.

If only our poor burghers could go home now, but it appears they are going to fight to the bitter end. I wonder if you saw Oom Paul's dispatch and the answer from England? When they [the British] take the country the Hollanders will have to find another hunting ground and they will never find another so favourable or so rich as this. It will be a blessing to be rid of those creatures as we have to thank them for much of our trouble,[104] but the English will bring in their beloved Cape darlings, Malays and coolies.[105] Good night. On Sunday it was just 5 months since we began this war and we have lived through centuries of trouble and care. We heard today that 90 of our men were killed and 240 wounded with Cronjé.[106] It is wonderful how our men were kept [in safety] in spite of the 110 guns and 70 000 English.

'The English are advancing ... Oh! the misery of this suspense'

A tense Pretoria waits as Lord Roberts marches from Bloemfontein towards the republican 'holy of holies': 13 March to 5 June 1900.

15 March [1900] I had another letter from William. He is weary of having to lie out in the veld for no one knows how long. They get no reliable news and have nothing to do but talk war from morning to evening. Poor boy.

Today Annie Frances[1] called and told us they had seen someone who was present when Cronjé surrendered. He says the burghers fought so bravely until their ammunition was destroyed by the enemy. It is a miracle they were not all killed with 110 guns firing on them. After they surrendered, our men shaved themselves and put on their best clothes and when they left for Cape Town they looked such a fine body of men. Oh! I am so glad! it almost broke my heart to think how those Cape Town niggers[2] would laugh and jeer at them because they would look so dirty and ragged, covered with mud and smoke after all those terrible days of hard fighting. After Cronjé had been taken away by Lord Roberts, old Mrs C mounted a horse and rode off to the English camp to see Lord R. She begged him to take her too because she said they were both old and had not many days to live. He granted her request. What a sight it must have been to see the dear old lady on horseback in her black dress and cappie![3] How the Tommies[4] must have stared. Lord R was very kind to our men and treated them so well. Bless him! we are grateful.

Things are getting darker and darker for us. The English are advancing from all sides. It is so hard to sit here day after day and wait for them to march in. Oh! what a bitter day it will be for Oom Paul and us all, when our flag will be hauled down and the Union Jack waves proudly out on the breeze. How they will cheer and sing 'God save the Queen' and how proud and grand and great they will feel because 105 000 of them have crushed a tiny handful of boers and stolen their birthright. My dear! when I think how these people have been worried into declaring war and now to have the English fling it into their faces, I get so mad!

Father sent a telegram to Kroonstad to hear how our uncle Jim is.[5] He is Under State Secretary for the OFS and we hoped that he had gone with the President to K[roonstad][6] but we received no answer. We can't find out anything about our brother Willie's family at Bethulie[7] either. It is so hard not to be able to hear how they are. The last thing we heard was that there was heavy fighting at Bethulie. Fancy, Oom Paul just escaped in time at Modder River. He was in the fighting lines and the English knew he was there. Just fancy how dreadful it would have been if they had taken the dear old boy. It is late, so good night.

Friday 16 [March 1900] There was such excitement here this morning when the officers [British prisoners of war] were sent off to their new quarters out of town.[8] I think they had nearly every cab in town to drive in. It was a piece of work to get all their luggage off. They look fine and well. Their prison life has certainly done them no harm. But we can't understand why they were not left where they were, seeing the whole place will soon belong to them.

I had backache again today but it was not as bad as usual. I read *Dombey and Son* while I had to lie down. Last week I finished *David Copperfield*.[9] I read it twice and am not tired of it even now. I wish I could tell old Dickens how I love his books and what a comfort the latter was to me. Many days when I was wretched about this war and felt sick of everything, I could forget it all and lose myself in David C. How full of humour and pathos he is and with what a master hand he draws each of his characters and makes them live and move before his readers. I am sure there never was another writer just like him. And what a firm belief he has in the good in mankind! You are not fond of his works, are you Sue? I wish you could read this book. I do not see how one can help enjoying it.

Father's eye has troubled him so much that he went to one of the new Dutch doctors. He says it is a growth in the eye but it must on no account be operated on as it will burst of itself. He gave him something to use, so I hope it will be alright.

It is hard to have to possess one's soul in patience. No wonder Longfellow[10] said that patience is godlike. Here we have to wait day after day to see how things will end. What tremendous changes there will be in every department of our Government. The educational system

Part 2: 'The English are advancing ...'

will be utterly changed. Our dear friend Dr Mansveld[11] will have to seek pastures new and all his bright band of greedy Hollanders with him. Much loss they will be! They caused all this bitterness and ill feeling and did their best to bring about war. I know there is the railway system[12] where more of our precious Hollanders will be cleared out and so on into all the different offices. Now I just wonder what they will do with all the officials. Surely they won't send them all off.

I do hope we will not have to leave this old house where we have lived such quiet peaceful lives for so many years.[13] Each room in this house is full of memories and we feel as if no other house can be as much to us as this one. Well, we must just wait and see. What we dread most is the demoralizing and degrading influence those soldiers will have on the natives and poor whites.[14] We expect 50 000 troops will be stationed here. Just think what a pest that will be. It makes me shudder to think that we will see sights here in our lovely Pretoria which are so common in Cape Town. Oh! that this curse might be kept from us for the sake of the innocent little children.[15]

RD Collins and his second wife, Carlie

18 March [1900] On Friday the officers were removed to their new quarters out of town. Of course our whole establishment turned out to see them ... Oh! I forgot I told you about the removal of the officers on Friday. I write to Lottie and William a little every day, so I some-times forget what I wrote to you. I wonder how long Lottie's letter will be by the time communication opens between Pretoria and Bethulie? It is so hard not to know how they are.

I wish that you could have heard Mr Bosman's sermon this morning. He has just returned from a visit to the front. He says he thought he knew his 'volk'[16] but he has been mistaken and is almost heartbroken at all the wicked things he saw and heard amongst them. At Volksrust[17] an official told him he found 20 000 cartridges in one man's waggon which he had stolen and was sending home ... another stole 60 000. He [Bosman] said is that not terrible and beastly to steal such holy things, because they are holy at this time when our Government cannot import more! They steal horses and anything they wish for, and the lies they tell are too awful. I [have] never heard such preaching in my life, the man seemed inspired. It was quite awful to sit and hear him pour it all out on us. He spared no one from Oom Paul to the least ... he laid our sins before us. He says he is convinced God is ready and willing to help in spite of the overwhelming numbers of the enemy but He cannot and dare not while our lives are full of corruption. When the war began we said our help is in God and the Mauser,[18] then it was Cronjé and the Mauser and now it is in the Mauser and God! ... and is it an[y] wonder that we have had these reverses? Once he almost groaned when he said, his voice hoarse with grief, 'Oh my people (volk) are a bad people full of corruption and sin. Sometimes I wonder if they are worthy of being spared!' This little minister of ours is the only man in the country who is not afraid to speak out and tell the people their sins. He is a grand man. If we had more like him there would be less corruption.

Today there are all sorts of whispers about a great victory over the enemy, but I am afraid it is false. Oom Paul returned from Kroonstad last night. We are always anxious when he is gone because they may capture him. Peace seems as far off as ever. Oh! dear. It is very curious that of all the number of babies born during the war, almost all are boys. A new generation of burghers!

Tuesday 20 [March 1900] The people seem very hopeful. I don't know why, because [the] Government keeps everything so quiet. Of course there are all sorts of rumours. These are some of them: 1400 prisoners are to be brought in on Wednesday; General Gatacre[19] and 400 troops captured; General Lord Roberts wounded and captured, and so on until one does not know what to believe. No wonder Mike du Toit declares David was on commando when he said: 'All men are liars!'

Sophia was so energetic today [that] she cleaned our bicycles while I was melting over our stove cooking the dinner.

22 March [1900] Oh! Sue child I am ashamed of being an Africander[20] and I am ashamed and broken hearted over my people. They are wicked and deceitful. I am afraid we do not deserve to be spared to become a

PART 2: 'The English are advancing ...'

nation. I daresay by this time you have heard that they have wrecked the coal mines in Natal.[21] Oh! I did not think our people could be so wicked and so utterly senseless. They had no right to be in Natal at all, and just think of the millions of pounds of damage that destruction means and all the loss to private people who never did us any harm. Now there will be hatred between N[atal] and Transvaal. What evil spirit could have advised that piece of devil's work? These wretched Hollanders must have had a hand in it. Even now when they know there is no chance for us, they are always egging the people on and stirring up bitterness and hate. It was an evil day for the country when these people came in.

In the last letter Mr vd Merwe wrote, he said [that] he thought he knew his people, but he learnt to know them in laager as they are, and they are wicked [and] full of meanness. They lie and steal and during the last terrible fight at Tugela only a few hundred did the fighting and when the order came to retreat, thousands came out [of hiding].[22] He could not believe his eyes. So you see how cowardly and mean they are. No wonder Mr Bosman is so downhearted. It is bitter to have to be ashamed of one's own people. One *Veldcornet* stole 60 horses from [the] Government. Many of the officers drink themselves drunk with the brandy sent by [the] Government to the front for the sick and wounded. Then they prate about their faith and say God will not let the English take the land. What must one do with such a wicked and deceitful people and oh! I do love them, the miserable wretches ...

After supper Your aunt called this morning. She was as bright as ever but does look so worn. I am so sorry for her and the daughters. It is a hard life for a frail woman to struggle on alone, especially during these times. They have only four boarders as all the men who can be spared are sent to the front.

25 March [1900] Mr Bosman had another of his straight talks this morning. If this nation does not become a model nation now, I am afraid they are beyond care. Yesterday we heard that a laager is being built for the women and children some miles out of town. If that is true, then I do not dare to think what horrors are before us.[23] We hear no news from the front at all. Child, every day we grow more weary of this awful war.

27 March [1900] Oh! Sue, there is another awful catastrophe for us. General Joubert is dying.[24] This evening in [the] meeting, auntie told us [that] Mr Bosman announced it. She says it came on the congregation like a thunder bolt. We all knew he was ill, but had no idea it was as bad. Doctor says he may go during the night. The people wept aloud and Mr B[osman] was so overcome he could hardly speak. Oh! what will become of us now? Oom Paul is with him. Ach! Why must this bitterness be added too, why must he go when there are others we can spare better. I would gladly give my life for his ... Good night.

1 April [1900] Our poor old general is resting quietly in his grave on his farm and we mourn the loss of a good and a wise man. His body was taken to the church for a short service before it was taken to the station. The heat was so great that we did not go, but we heard that it was one of the biggest processions ever seen here. There were hundreds of beautiful wreaths. The English officers sent a very fine one, someone said it cost £40, but we do not believe it. We had sacrament today. I wonder how it will be with our tempest-torn land when the next sacrament comes?

We have [had] such terribly hot days that we all look quite washed out. Yesterday we heard of a great victory, but as we are not sure I will not tell you until we hear officially.

2 April [1900] We had a little rain. It is a relief to have a little cool weather again. At sewing class Mrs v Alphen[25] told us about our poor old general's last hours. She says he was delirious all the time and waved all away even his poor wife, and fancied he was commanding the burghers in battle. At 11 o'clock that night he died and they laid him in the sitting room where they sat with him and his broken hearted old wife the whole night. Mrs v A[lphen] says it was awful to see her grief. She would not keep away from him but would go and clasp her arms around his body. They were married almost 50 years and she always went with him on commando. They say the officers' wreath was most beautiful. They [also] sent Mr Bosman £30 for the poor!!

Commandant General Joubert

Part 2: 'The English are advancing ...'

23 April [1900] So much has happened since I last wrote. Carlie has a son.[26] We had a very anxious time. She took ill on Saturday night at 12 o'clock and baby only came on Monday afternoon at 3.30, and then Doctor had to use instruments. She suffered fearfully and was almost gone, but the baby is such a splendidly healthy boy that she is repaid tenfold. We call him Buller until he gets his own name. He was born on the 9th of this month and ought to be a man of peace as he was born under the Red Cross. Carlie has a splendid nurse. We are all so fond of her. She is only 31 and has had first rate training. She is so bright and full of fun. Her name is Odette Gardhuizen. But I will tell you more about her another day, as my back is worrying me.

William was home for almost 2 weeks. They sent him to Vryheid to take the place of Public Prosecutor[27] for two months. It is a rest not to have to worry about him.

26 April [1900] We had such a pleasant surprise yesterday, our brother Willie turned up unexpectedly. We have been so anxious about him and were afraid that the English had captured him. He had a very narrow escape and got off to Kroonstad. He came here with the Treasurer General of the Free State and left again this evening. He heard that Lottie and the children escaped to our grandmother's[28] farm, so they are safe. We are very anxious about him because he is to be sent on a very dangerous mission. I have not heard father laugh as he did at dinner today, since the war began, at some of Will's funny experiences.

I suppose you have by this time heard of that horrible explosion of the bomb factory[29] at Johannesburg. People say there was foul play. How all our reverses seem to come on us at once. Today we heard all sorts of bad news about a dreadful defeat and hundreds of our people killed, but there is no official report.[30] Child! Child! there seems no hope ... for a little while we began to be hopeful because we have had a few victories, but now everything goes against us again.

Something awful has just happened. Sophia and I were playing draughts when father came in and said a man had been stabbed in the street and was brought here. He has just died. Is it not horrible?

Sunday 6 May [1900] This has not been a peaceful Sabbath at all. The town is so full of unrest and trouble. Early in the day we heard that the English had taken Winburg and Fourteen Streams.[31] This afternoon all the men from 16 to 60 [years of age] had to appear on the Church

Square and received an order to leave for the front tomorrow. You can imagine the excitement.

We all feel that we are very near the end. One more stand and all will be over. Our hearts are heavy. We fear the worst. The men are so weary and faint hearted that we do not even know whether their officers will get them to make a last stand.[32] Child, child, we have lived through bitter anxious days, and long with unspeakable longing for peace, but oh! the bitterness of the thought that all the sorrow and heartbreak has been in vain. How can we who truly love the country, bear to see those terrible English march into our lovely Pretoria and hoist their flags. It seems too hard that they are always allowed to take what they want. And how they can be proud of such a victory – 102 000 against our little handful of untrained men? Ach! ach, if we could all go away, far away where the English will never trouble us again. They say they will make a present of the two states to their Queen on her birthday. May the gift bring her much happiness. It was gained at the cost of thousands of broken hearted women, and the blood of our best and bravest men has been shed; hundreds of happy homes have been ruined and made desolate. Surely it is a costly gift, but a curse will go with it!

This afternoon little Buller was christened Richard Hugo. Poor little chap, what troublous times he has come in. I wonder what he will have to live through? Auntie, uncle and the girls were present and we had quite a family gathering, but all the time our hearts were full of anxiety. We dread every day now. The Government keeps things so quiet that we never know what is happening. Our brother Willie was here again with some of the OF State officials. We fancy they brought some of their documents for safekeeping, but he would not let out anything to us. It is 2 months since he saw his family.

There is much talk over a blind child in Johannesburg who is said to have foretold that explosion and several other things. We are to have more explosions, a bloody battle on 24 May, peace on 4th of June and soon after that Oom Paul is to depart this life.

8 May [1900] No more news from the front. We are just waiting for the end. The whole of the civilized world is awaiting the end with breathless interest and there is not one power which will lift a finger to stop this unrighteous war. Oh! these two tiny brave little republics, they have strained every nerve and now they are lying bleeding just waiting for the great mighty English nation to proclaim them as her own. Our *V[olks]raad* opened yesterday, I suppose for the last time.[33]

Dear Sue, I thought so much about you. Do you know that this is the first time for about 18 years that I have not sent you a birthday greeting?[34] I however wished you all manner of good wishes, and how I longed to see your dear face. Today we heard that our people had taken Mafeking, but we don't believe it.[35] Oh, I forgot to tell you, Sophia had such a lovely birthday. The day was flooded with sunshine and our friends sent her beautiful flowers, and she got other presents too.

Sunday 13 May [1900] It is such an ideal Sabbath. Calm and quiet but oh! what scenes of horror there must be in the F[ree] State. We heard there was heavy fighting and Kroonstad had been taken.[36] Rev Bosman had an earnest address and made a stirring appeal to the Africander women to encourage the men to fight.[37] He admits that only a miracle can save us but believes that if our men stand by each other, help may yet come. I cannot see the use of shedding more blood and only long for this awful war to cease. It is getting unendurable to sit here day after day and wait for those English to come.

We have lived in this state of unrest for 7 months now. It has told on father. He looks so worn and has lost his appetite. We are so anxious about him. Baby has been very fretful too and Carlie does not seem to gain much strength. She can do nothing except attend to the child and the least thing makes her sick. The fever is so bad this year. In some districts whole families have died.

Sunday 20 May [1900] Dear Sue, just a few lines. I am writing this in our bedroom. As I had a dose of my usual backache I did not go to church but spent the morning in bed and longing to hear news from the front. Oh! the misery of this suspense. We just live a day at a time and never know what will become of us. We may be ordered out to laager any day.[38] Johannesburg is in a state of panic because the English are marching on to it and the poor people do not know what [the] Government intends doing. Those hateful Hollanders urge them to have the mines blown up[39] and the people in power are so utterly mad that there is no knowing what they will do. Women and children are fleeing from both Johannesburg and Pretoria.[40] Many of the people wish for peace at any price before the country is utterly ruined, but Oom Paul refuses.[41] We expect a battle at Irene.[42] That is to say, if the burghers will make a last stand, because they are so weary and downhearted that lately they have always fled seeing that there are 50 soldiers to one burgher! We all pray that peace may be made so that we [will] be saved from the horrors of laager life. Just think what it will mean for a lot of women and young children to be huddled in tents in mid-winter, with little food and in constant dread of what may be.

You can imagine how troubled we all are. [The] Government will not let out anything. We only know the enemy is coming. We do not even know the names of the killed and wounded. Our brother Will, we have lost sight of again. Yesterday we received this telegram from William: 'Post closed, office closed. Will remain here until the enemy is near.' I told you he was in Vryheid. Well, we heard they had decided to surrender the district because the country there is too flat to make good positions. Now that must have happened and yet they give us no official notice. We have no idea where William is or what he will do. Good night.

Sunday 27 May [1900] We are still waiting for the end and we had hoped that by this time it would all have been ended. I am just reminded of the closing lines of Evangeline:

> 'All was ended now, the hope and the fear and the sorrow,
> All the aching void of heart, and the restless longing,
> All the dull, deep pain and constant anguish of patience.'

The women of OFS and Transvaal know what the anguish of patience means. We heard that the English are through the Vaal [River] but further we know absolutely nothing. It is too bad that we are kept in such ignorance. The rats are leaving the sinking ship – the Hollanders have left by dozens – by that we know there is no hope. Food is so scarce that there is a rumour that the prisoners will be put over the border. Meal is over £3 a bag and flour £2. 5s. I have no idea where our brother Willie is, or William. They may both be dead. Oh! will we ever be able to forget the sorrow this horrible war has caused. Every day we see and hear of more. Our hearts ache for those unfortunate Colonial people who were dragged into it.[43] There are hundreds of them. They do not know what will become of them when the English get here. There are two of our mother's cousins. The one was to have been shot but before the time our people retook the town and so he escaped. I believe our Government made them an offer to send them to Holland but what are they to do there? Everything is such a hopeless muddle that I wonder sometimes how it is ever to be put straight. Now it is almost 8 months.

PART 2: 'The English are advancing ...'

Tuesday 29 [May 1900] At last the end is in sight. Pretoria is in an intense state of nervous excitement. Child, it is awful. We can settle to nothing. Father has been out three times already (and it is not 11o'clock yet) to try and get news. Every time he comes in he tells more bad news. They say there has been heavy fighting and those English are in Johannesburg.[44] Our hearts ache for the poor anxious women and our weary burghers. General L Botha[45] said there would be awful fighting today. There is a report that some burghers and their wives looted the commissariat in Johannesburg last night. I suppose the poor people are so desperate now that they don't care what they do. People here are very anxious and are trying to get a corps of 500 men to guard the town[46] because there is a report that our Government is going to leave for Lydenburg,[47] so we will be left to surrender ourselves to the British! I don't know what madness is moving them to that step. They might as well give in, there is no hope. We heard 300 of our people were killed yesterday, but hope it is not true.[48]

Commandant General Louis Botha

Oh! to think that it is almost over and we will soon be British subjects and never sing our *Volkslied*[49] again. This horrible war, what ruin and destruction and suffering it has cost us all. I can't tell you how we feel today. There seems to be nothing for us but just to wait in utter despair until they march in tomorrow.[50] Why, oh why, must the English get everything they want? Now that hateful Rhodes will come here and do what he pleases, and how they will all lord it over us and there are those poor Colonial rebels. Where will they fly to, and there are 1000. I am too wretched to write more.

31 May [1900] Did you think that the day would come when we would pray for the speedy arrival of the English into Pretoria? Well, it has come. Yesterday Pretoria woke to find that its Government had gone and left us all in the lurch. All the gold had disappeared[51] as well as all the ammunition and a tremendous quantity of food. So here we are with no head, no police and no orders left to any officials as to what we are expected to do. To make matters worse the officials have not been paid and during the war all the salaries have been reduced. To say the feelings of the people towards Oom Paul and the rest are bitter, does not in the least express it. All rushed to the bank to get that wretched paper money changed, but they refused to do it.[52]

Today the excitement was even greater – the climax was reached when the government stores were looted.[53] Mr Voss says it was an awful sight to see the women rush in and carry off as much as they could. Waggons and carts were loaded with meal, tea, coffee and so on and there was no one to stop them. There were hundreds of armed burghers who helped in this disgraceful affair instead of stopping it.[54]

Ach! child we were so heart-sore over it all. To think that our government could serve us such a mean trick. It is a blot on the whole nation. The English have taken Johannesburg and now instead of letting them come and take possession here we hear that there is to be a battle at Six Mile Spruit[55] tomorrow. I do hope the burghers will not stand – what is the use? There is no chance.

4 June [1900] ... Just a few lines. We can hear the cannon fire. It sounds like thunder. Oh! Sue our hearts are full of anxiety. We do not know what will happen before tonight. It is coming nearer and nearer and we are so afraid the boers will retreat into Pretoria, then the English will bombard it, and think of all the hundreds of women and little children. I am living with the Voss family for the present.[56] Mrs

The looting of the government stores in Pretoria

PART 2: 'The English are advancing ...'

British troops march into Pretoria along Market Street

Voss is Miss du Toit's sister. You will understand how anxious I feel if I tell you she is to be confined next month. The whole morning I have been praying God to prevent the bombardment for the sake of such women. I can't write ... God help us, it is coming so near.

9. 30 [pm] ... It is all over ... Pretoria belongs to England! Child, I can never tell you how we felt today when the bombs came nearer and nearer. Some burst in Sunnyside[57] and several of the ladies fled into town. Two [shells] are said to have burst near the lunatic asylum[58] and one near the Volks Hospital.[59] At 5 o'clock an English officer[60] came in with a white flag and demanded our surrender or else to have the place bombarded. The burghers did nothing but retreat, so what could we do but surrender? Besides, what is the use of going on when our miserable Government has deserted us. I can't tell you how humiliated we feel by the disgrace which Oom Paul and his whole set have brought on us. They coined more money during the last few days and we all hoped it was to pay the officials and this morning we heard that Smuds,[61] the State Attorney went off with it. Where, no one knows. Oh! the people are just mad against Oom Paul and wish the burghers would all go to their homes. Tomorrow, I suppose the troops will march in.

5 June [1900] This afternoon the troops marched in thousands. It was a sight we will never forget. There seemed no end to them.[62] They say they will spare no pains to get Oom Paul.

Lord Roberts and the British troops take the salute as the Union Jack is raised on the Government Buildings on Church Square Pretoria on 5 June 1900. (From a comtemporary sketch by Melton Prior that appeared in a supplement to the Illustrated London News *of 21 June 1900)*

'... Pretoria belongs to England!'
The town under British control, June 1900 to June 1902. From the arrival of Lord Roberts to 'peace ... at last!'

12 June [1900] It is just 8 days since these dreadful troops came pouring in in thousands and it seems years and years. Mrs Voss is just busy reading their first *Government Gazette*. It does seem so strange to read 'God save the Queen' instead of 'God bless land and people'. Ach! Sue! to think that they are right here in our lovely Pretoria and have the right to do what they will. They have published their Martial Law and they enforce [it] very strictly.[1] We are all to be in our houses by 7 o'clock [pm]. Of course no church can have [a] service in the evening on that account, so we have [an] afternoon service instead. No one is allowed to ride their bicycles without a permit and they refuse permits to almost all except doctors and ministers.

One good thing they have done is to leave the Native Law unchanged.[2] As soon as the niggers heard that the English were coming they became dreadfully cheeky and tore up their passes and rode their bicycles and marched about on the sidewalks and crowed over us.[3] Oh! it was hateful. Well, the English promptly quenched them in a manner which they did not at all enjoy.

When we saw that tremendous host march in last week we thought the war was ended but our poor burghers have still been having fights[4] and they have killed hundreds of English. Today we heard that French[5] has had to go back to the OFS, as communication has been cut off by our people. We wish they would all just lay down their arms – what is the use of prolonging this wretched war because they are buying up all the food [and] we will soon have none left.

I am very happy with the Vosses, they are such dear friends of ours.[6] The eldest daughter is at school in Wellington. [At home] there are two boys and one little girl. They are very nice, bright children. The eldest boy, George, is 16 and is a strong Transvaler. Little Vivian is a lovely boy of 6. He is a cause of great amusement to us all. He is

Thomas Voss

an enthusiastic burgher and always prays: 'Lord, make our burghers strong and give us a big victory!' Cathie[7] is a fair haired girl of 8, we share a room and I teach her music. She makes a fine pupil.

Our house is a good half hour's walk from Mrs Voss' house[8] and now that I can't ride I find it impossible to go home often. I was there yesterday. Buller[9] did not look well, but the others were all right. The hospital is crowded with English officers and the School has been turned into a hospital for soldiers.[10]

14 June [1900] There are all sorts of wild rumours around. We heard that our people had a great victory and killed hundreds of English and captured about 1200 waggons and destroyed [a] great many bombs![11] Mrs Voss heard from an officer that things were looking very bad for them. French was obliged to go back to the OFS. Of course we get in no news, but then they do not either as our people have cut off all communication from them. We know for a fact that they can't get food, because they have commandeered all the provisions from the shops and now they are going to search the private houses and will only allow us enough provisions for 1 month!

You have no idea how it feels to be cut off from all the world even from our own districts because now we do not even get news from Johannesburg. The post and telegraph offices are closed. All the men are out of work and as [the] Government never paid them for the last month, you can understand in what a state almost all the families are. Some have no money and no food and here this wretched war is dragging on endlessly. Heaven only knows what is to become of us all.

To crown it all, we heard that the plague has broken out in Buller's force.[12] [A]round and in Pretoria the English have 11 000 sick and wounded. In the Model School there are 150 ill and the hospital is full too. On one of the hills they have a hospital camp for the hundreds of sick horses. Oh! the misery and sorrow of this awful time, who can describe it?

We have had no news from my brother or William and I suppose we will have none until the war is over. I went home yesterday

PART 3: '... Pretoria belongs to England!'

afternoon. Father's eye is very painful and he is heartbroken over all the sorrow and misery. He sees a lot of it, as he is secretary to the Red Cross. Baby does not seem very bright. There is a Duke in the hospital ... grand, isn't it? Four of their Lords were killed this week. Good night.

Sunday 17 June [1900] Still this weary war continues. Dear! will the day ever come when we will have peace? On Friday night I dreamed peace was proclaimed and we were so relieved at the terrible load lifted from our hearts that we wept for joy ... but what a disappointment it was to wake and find it was only a dream. It was very cold and windy today. Helen[13] and I had supper at home tonight and to our surprise it began to rain hard [at] about 5.30 [pm]. As we had to be in by 7 o'clock we had to rush down as fast as possible. We did not enjoy the long walk in the cold and wet but we had a nice time at home. I wish you could see how lovely our flowers looked. We have violets, daisies, marigolds, pinks, carnations and phlox.

The streets were just crowded with soldiers. I heard that the day they marched in there were 50 000 and a few days later 50 000 more came. One of the nurses from the Volks Hospital said this morning that the hospital is crowded with soldiers and they are all half starved when they are brought [in], and have high fever. She says the nurses are all heartbroken by all the misery they see, and the tales of terrible suffering they hear. The soldiers say the forced marching they have had to do has been killing, then they had hardly any food. Many of their companions just dropped out and were left to die in the veld if they could not care for them! They have fever in the worst form and die by the hundreds here. She says it is awful to see them, their tongues are black and their lips blue and cracked with fever and they are covered with insects! The first thing they ask for is food. 1100 were left sick of fever in Bloemfontein and in Pretoria there are 1000 wounded, besides hundreds down with fever.[14] Oh! it is too awful. Who will have to pay for all this horrible suffering? One of the sick soldiers said the burghers are fighting like devils now!

We are getting so short of things. Coal sells at 10/- and 15/- a bag and wood can't be had; food too, is getting very scarce. The English don't seem able to get in supplies either, as our people have broken up the line again. Ach! I am sick to my soul of all this miserable business. I wonder where William is? Today it was 25 days since we [last] heard from him. Good night, Sue.

27 June [1900] We are still shut in, and are in fact little better than prisoners.[15] No one is allowed out of Pretoria except on permit, which by the way is granted to very few. Every night at seven the town is deserted until 6.30 [am] the next day. Mr Voss had hard work to get a night permit and did not succeed until he got a certificate from the doctor as to the reason why, and now he will only be allowed to keep it for 3 weeks and if Mrs Voss' little affair[16] does not come off during that time, he is to have it renewed. I tried to get a permit for riding my bicycle but was refused because I do not need it for business! I was so disgusted at the behaviour of that creature who gives out permits, I felt inclined to shake him.

Oh! these conceited English, how we detest them. One of their officers said to a lady into whose garden he had turned their horses, that we Dutch women were much too cheeky and needed to be put down. That was all she got for asking him to remove the horses. Several houses have been broken open and the furniture destroyed. Of course when our people complain, Lord Roberts always says bring the soldier who is guilty and I will punish him, but who is to point out the right man amongst thousands of their Khakies who all look alike. I can tell you they make us feel that we must bend. They are very great on proclamations and oaths. Oh! we are sick of it all and long to hear how our poor men at the front are getting on. It is too awful to go on day after day and never hear a single bit of news. How we wonder what the great busy world is doing. We do not even get news from Johannesburg although they say the post is open! We have not seen a newspaper for a month. Only their *Government Gazette*. We are not allowed to wear our colours and some ladies were stopped in the streets and their colours taken off! I don't know whether I told you that Mr v Broekhuizen[17] our assistant minister was imprisoned because he refused to take the oath of neutrality.[18] They let him out after 10 days because the ladies sent a memorial to Lord R, praying them to set him free. He says the prison fare was awful: mealie pap[19] cooked by kaffirs[20] in dirty pots with dirty water.

Lord Roberts

28 [June 1900] Sophia spent the day with us. It was so nice to have her. The Vosses are very, very good

PART 3: '... Pretoria belongs to England!'

to me and I am quite happy here. If only this awful war was ended. The English have started a newspaper and have the imprudence to call it *The Pretoria Friend*.[21]

9 July [1900] We are still shut in and its seems as if we will always remain in this delightful state. Ach! I don't care, I only wish we were all dead. There is no news from William. Father has had orders to clear out of the house where we have lived for 11 years. They want the whole [building] for a hospital. They have however given [him] another house in which we can live as long as this awful war lasts.[22] They are to move next week. It is a mercy we have not to pay rent[23] as father has only about £100 to live on and nothing coming in.

Mrs Voss has a lovely little girl, it was born on Friday. I have my hands full and am as busy as possible. I am thankful for the work because I don't want time to think. Oh! I am so sorry to leave our garden. It looks so lovely with all the flowers. And that dear old house in which we have been so happy – each room is full of memories.[24] Well, after all there are better mansions higher up. Good night, dear.

22 July [1900] The post is said to be open to the Colony but we receive very few letters. I wonder why you don't write? We are shocked to hear of Wally's death. Your poor aunt has had sorrow and trouble enough in her life.

My people have been in their new home for almost three weeks. It must have been a beautiful house in its day but has been dreadfully neglected and was awfully dirty. The grounds are large and there is plenty of room. I am still staying with Mrs Voss. She does not move about yet and I am kept very busy, but I am only too glad to have my hands full. You remember the nurse I told you was with Carlie when Buller came, well she is with Mrs Voss and I have learnt to know her pretty well.[25]

We hear no news from the front. Only now and then we hear the cannon fire. It is strange that with all their great host they [the British] are unable to put an end to the war. We hear they are getting out more troops! They have been quite busy the last few days in putting our dear friends the Hollanders over the border.[26]

2 September [1900] It is more than a month since I wrote the above. I have been too weary and heart sore about this endless war to write. We are just <u>enduring</u> and praying for the end. Sometimes it seems too bitter even for us to pray, yet to whom can we carry our stricken, heavy hearts if not to the great 'All Father'? Child, we have lived through oceans of sorrow and trouble, many of us, and yet we have much to be thankful for. We have learnt lessons during this dark time which could never have been taught [to] us in any other way. Now we know what poor weak, defiled mortals we really are and all the riches and prosperity was very bad for us. We became so selfish and corrupt that we were as a people sinking fast, and this sharp lesson had to be sent to save us. Oh! that it were but ended and that our poor people may come out purified.

I suppose you people have all heard about the 'Great Plot of Cordua'[27] and his execution. I wonder how it struck you? To us, who have lived in the same town and knew him, it is very pitiful and makes our hearts bleed to think of it and then those hateful newspapers say: 'We are glad to hear he has been shot because we <u>feared</u> the sentence would not be carried out!'

He came of a wealthy Danish[28] family and was only 23, a fair-faced enthusiastic boy. He, like so many of our artillery officers who were in town when the English came, was let out on parole. He could not get funds from home and fell into bad company and was tempted to drink. That mean sneak Gano,[29] an English spy, led him on and plied him with drink and by all sorts of hints and insinuations, at last led the poor boy on to form a plot and told him he would give him a pass to go to the boer lines and he, Gano, would also join them. Well, they left town but when Cordua became sober he wished to return as he said he did not want to break his parole and get Major Erasmus,[30] who was responsible for him, into trouble. That devil Gano refused and always urged him on. The next day they were arrested.

Hans Cordua

The trial lasted about 3 days and in the evidence it all came out clearly that this unfortunate boy had just been led on by Gano who really formed the plot. The jury declared him [Cordua] guilty and we all felt quite sure he would be imprisoned for some years. Imagine our horror when the next day it was reported that they shot the poor boy at 7 o'clock that morning. Oh! it was too bitterly sad. We cried over him as if he was our own brother. To think of a young life cut off in the bloom of its strength and life is so sweet and fair at 23.

Mrs Erasmus had been very kind to him and took him into their home when he had no more money. She is crushed by it and has grown quite old-looking. Her husband Major E was imprisoned for 12 days and then sent to Ceylon[31] for no earthly reason but that they suspected him too, on account of Cordua. Yesterday she came and gave Mrs v der Spuy[32] a full account of the poor boy's end as her husband told it her before he left.

His cell was next [to] Cordua's and they could speak to each other through the partition. The night before, an officer came into Major's cell and said: 'Come with me, I must tell C[ordua] he is to be shot!' Major, half stunned, went. C rose as they entered and the officer said: 'It is my sad duty to tell you [that] you are to be shot tomorrow at 7!' C never uttered a word but the look of despair and anguish on his face was heartbreaking. The officer seemed deeply moved himself and said 'Is there anything I can do for you?' but the poor boy never answered a word. Then they left [and] as the door closed he cried out 'Major! Major! come to me' and oh! Sue, they would not even allow the boy that drop of comfort! They sent the chaplain and jailor and they remained with him the whole of that terrible last night. The chaplain said he prayed and spoke to him but all the time he only said 'I am too stunned, I can't take it in.' He spoke to Major off and on, telling him of different things he wished him to attend to. As the time drew near Major said 'Hansie are you still there?' 'Yes Major, but it is only 10 minutes now. The whole night I have been counting the minutes.' Seven o'clock struck. They led him out. The soldiers stood ready. The volley was fired and Cordua's young life was ended. Major E cried like a child the whole day and could not be comforted. Oh! I think it is the most tragic thing I have ever heard and we are very sad about it. What it must mean to his widowed mother away in Europe. Mrs E was allowed to read the letter he wrote to his mother. If Lord Roberts had saved his life it would have done much towards gaining the respect of our people.

They have put hundreds of our people over the border – some who were quite innocent and they were not even told why they were put over. Pretoria is getting quite empty and no one feels safe. We have to be so careful what we say or do.[33] Our food is getting very low and there are no groceries to be had in the shops. Many families live on mealie pap. Meat is very lean and poor at 2/- a lb. Now we even

General Christiaan de Wet

enjoy dry bread and smile to think of the days when we refused to eat certain jams because we did not fancy them! Jams are unheard of luxuries now, so are butter and milk.

They are still chasing De Wet.[34] Last week about four generals with thousands of soldiers were after him and still they let him slip through. We are proud of him – even they admire him. Goodnight Sue.

19 September [1900] Father has had a relapse and is very wretched. I was shocked to see how bad he looked this afternoon when I went home. General Botha is very ill.[35] I wonder if that will have any effect on matters? Our food is very scarce and we can't get wood or coal. Today a little coal came in but there was such a rush that if three times the same quantity had come, it would not have been enough.

22 Sept[ember 1900] Ach! I am weary of life. The world is so wretchedly full of sorrow and pain. Wherever you turn, there is fresh trouble. Poor little Vivie[36] has been ill with scarlet fever for three days. Tonight he is worse. It is pitiful to see how this fever is burning away his strength. Dear little chap. He was so bright and full of life the day before and now he lies there so weak and helpless. Mrs Voss is terribly anxious but is as calm and sweet as ever. I have my hands full with all the housework and Dorothy.[37] Fortunately she is very good. I only hope she and the other two children won't take it. The heat today was intense. Of course I don't go home now for fear of carrying the infection but So and Helen come and visit me at the gate. Father is better. Good night.

Sunday morning, 23 Sept[ember 1900] During the night Vivie was so bad that Mrs Voss thought that he was dying. Doctor says it is a malignant form of scarlet fever. We are all forbidden to go into the room. Mrs Voss is not to handle Dorothy. We are going to get Nurse Gardhuizen (you remember I told you about her) to come and attend to her, because she is a delicate little thing and I have as much as I can do with the housekeeping. The house is so quiet and we all feel so depressed and wretched. Poor little Vivie! We dare not think of what the end may be. On Tuesday it was just 5 years since his little sister Lena died. She was the loveliest child I ever saw.

PART 3: '... Pretoria belongs to England!'

Wednesday 26 [September 1900] It seems ages since last Thursday when dear little Vivie took ill. Sunday night we thought he was going, but now he is getting on nicely. Dorothy is very ill. During the night, nurse thought she was dying. Poor little Dot. She looks like a snowflake. I don't know what on earth we would do without nurse. She is so splendid with the little one. Yesterday my dear sister came to see me at the gate and I feel as unhappy about her, she does look wretchedly ill herself. Oh! if only our own dear mother[38] were here I would not worry about her, because then I would know she was well cared for. Sue, child you must love and cherish your mother while you have her.[39] ...

... The heat is awful and the town is just full of sickness. Ach! life is very sad and I am so dead tired of it all. How I wish So and I could go to mother. We are not needed in our home any more.

27 [September 1900] The heat is awful. If I did not have such a lot of work to do and had time to sit down and think about it, I would just collapse because I don't know when I felt the heat as much as this year. Our feet are so painful at night partly on account of the great heat, also because there are no soft house-shoes or slippers to be had in the town. You would be astonished to see with what broken shoes we go about but what [else] can we do? There is some talk in town of our getting in food supplies next week but seeing is believing, so we don't put any faith in that. Today we heard that the line had been broken up between us and Middelburg. What in the name of all that is ridiculous, the whole host of England is doing that they can't stop this wretched war, I don't know. To judge by the thousands of Khakies roaming about the streets, one would say that England has been cleared of all the men and still they can't crush a handful of boers.

28 Sept[ember 1900] I do feel so disgusted and ashamed of our women because of the way they carry on with these Khakies. Of the poorer classes I don't speak – we expected them to do it, but that the better class should do it and many of their husbands and brothers are still fighting.[40] Now there is a woman like Mrs L Botha. She always has a lot of officers about her. It does show such bad taste, to say the least.[41] As for the young girls it is disgusting how they lay themselves out to attract these officers. No wonder poor Mr Bosman is so heartsore over it all.

By the bye, he has had such sorrow lately. They received a telegram telling Mrs Bosman that Anna, their second daughter, was dangerously ill in the Colony. She had to leave by the next train. Of course she will not be allowed to return until the war is over, and who knows how long that will be. It was dreadfully hard for Mr B to be without her at this time when he needs her most.

Last week the English brought in 160 families whose homes they [had] burned. Goodness knows what they will do with these poor people after the war. Oh! The awful ruin and desolation in the country! They say all the farms around Pretoria have been destroyed.[42] Yesterday afternoon I rode out and So met me, so we had a chat in the Park.[43] Dorothy is a little better, Vivie is getting on too. He still has the most awful legs – if they don't itch they ache and if they don't ache they itch.

2 October [1900] Great joy in the town, the provisions came in at last! The shops were stormed and at last the doors were locked and only four people let in at a time! It was quite funny to see almost every other person march off with a pkt [packet] of candles. It shows what we endured for the want of light. Oh! These weary months, I wonder how we lived through them. If only we had peace now. Vivie is getting better but baby, I am afraid, is slipping away.[44] Sweet, wee thing. She came like a pale ray of sunshine and stayed just long enough to make us all love her. Good night, Sue.

5 Oc[tober 1900] I am dead tired tonight. Our boy ran off again.[45] That means I had to do all the work. At 2.30 [pm] I finished in the kitchen and at 3 I had to be at the dentist. I do not mind the work but when it comes to washing the pots and the dishes after dinner, I get awfully sad. On Sunday I worked like mad (excuse the elegant expression) and there seemed no end to all the pots and the dishes. You would have laughed to have seen Georgie, Kathie and I washing baby's nappies in the bathroom. We had quite a washing party. K washes beautifully, and so does G, for a boy. Vivie got up today and is doing well, but baby is very miserable.

Yesterday I got a letter from William but it was four months old. The English asked father to take charge of a school but I am afraid he will not be able to do it.

6 Oc[tober 1900] Today the work is not quite as much as we have a great lumbering kaffir girl.[46] She is a stupid but can at least carry the

PART 3: '... Pretoria belongs to England!'

coal and wash the dishes. You see, Sue, I have learnt to be grateful for small mercies! I do wish I could just show you nurse's slippers as a sample of the state to which our shoes are reduced. They were green cloth originally, now they are just a patchwork of holes and stitches. It is amusing to see her put in a few fresh stitches every morning. I do wish they would let us get in shoes if nothing else. One of the shoe shops which had been closed was opened on Tuesday and there was a tremendous rush. The doors were locked and only a few people let in at a time. One lady who was almost barefooted, was obliged to pay £1. 4s for a pair marked 11/-.

Pretoria is sweet with all the roses. Every garden is full of them and it is a pleasure to ride slowly along and see all the lovely colours.

10 Oc[tober 1900] Poor Oom Paul's birthday. We thought much about him and wondered where he is.[47] It is hard that in his old age he is a fugitive.

We are still having a dreary time with poor Dorothy. She is just wasting away. Tonight she is very fretful. Mrs Voss looks dreadfully worn and ill herself. Tomorrow it will be a year since war was declared.

12 Oc[tober 1900] My dear, the pleasure of receiving your letters yesterday! I posted one to you today and hope you will receive it. Our poor people are still fighting. Last Monday there was heavy fighting at Six Mile Spruit. We could hear the cannon. If only we could get lists of our killed and wounded, but this silence is so trying. The English are all mad on curios. They buy our pennies at 2/6! And there is quite a rush for stamps. One of their doctors has a gold ring with De Wet's name on it. A soldier who was present when they burnt his house, looted it and gave it to him.

We are so anxious about William because we had hoped that he had laid down his arms.[48] We cannot understand why our people go on fighting when it is such a hopeless case and the country is being utterly ruined.

15 Oc[tober 1900] Some more people are to go over the border. Mrs Honey, [Mrs] Armstrong and Mrs Malan,[49] daughter of our dear old General Joubert, are the three we heard who have to go. I wonder what they said? Ach! these English and their talk of fair play and justice! We heard that during the fighting last week they lost heavily and 160 wounded came in. Of course from them we never hear a word to the credit of our people. We have given up all hope of having peace even by Christmas. The people are all being flooded with old letters. Mrs Voss received about 40 during the last few days. I got one 2 months old.

16 [October 1900] Tomorrow it is our dear mother's birthday. What lovely memories we have of her and what joy to think that some day we will see her again. The [railway] line is broken up between us and Durban. They have forbidden the refugees to return [and] that means that this war will drag on for months. Oh! child I do feel so utterly heartsick and feel that I cannot bear this suspense for another month. If we could but hear from William!

22 October [1900] We heard this morning that Botha is near Pretoria and a big battle was expected. I don't think it came off because we did not hear the cannon. They are still chasing De Wet. It almost seems as if they will spend another year over it. Dear! dear! I wonder if we will live to see the end of this war. Father and Johannes vd Merwe are teaching the children of the poor people whom the English brought in some weeks ago. They have about 40 pupils.[50] We are longing to hear from William and our brother. It is so dreadful to think that something may have happened to them and we will not hear about it.

We also heard that Oom Paul sailed on Saturday. We were thankful because more provisions came in – we were again almost out of supplies as there was such a rush when the first lot came in, that nobody could lay in a large supply. We are so anxious for the soft goods to come. Many of the children can't attend S[unday] School as they have no shoes. Georgie Voss had to remain at home too, so as to get his shoes mended!

2 November [1900] We have had such beautiful rain since last night and it is so cold that we have a fire in the dining room! Our thoughts go out to our poor burghers away in the veld, perhaps without tents or food. Oh, what can possess them to go on fighting? By what we hear it seems they are fast losing all sense of right feeling and this war is no longer fair fighting but just a series of raiding parties. Small commandos sneak out and plunder wherever they can and when the English come, they vanish. The misery of it all. Our people will be little better than highway robbers if all we hear is true. The English manage to keep things so quiet that we have no idea how things are.

PART 3: '... Pretoria belongs to England!'

We however heard that there were two great battles this week and they lost heavily.[51]

Mr Voss got Mrs Voss and myself to go and see the funeral of Prince Christian.[52] We did not like the idea because it was at 9.30 [am]. I had the bread rising and the dinner had to be cooked and Mrs Voss had Dorothy to attend to, but Mr Voss had a cab waiting and would have us go. Georgie took charge of baby and I left the bread to take care of itself. We waited until 12.15 [pm] before the procession passed. But it was well worth waiting for. There were thousands and thousands of soldiers and it was a grand sight to see them march past. Ach! if they had only been our own people, how proud we would have been of them. The coffin was covered with their flag. His helmet rested on it and his splendid horse was led after the gun [carriage] on which he was carried to the cemetery. Is it not strange that a prince should be resting in our cemetery! How many of her best and bravest England has had to lose in Africa. As soon as the procession passed we rushed off for a cab and came home to find baby just beginning to get fretful and the bread was in the oven – our boy, for a wonder, attended to it.

One store got in shoes this week, you can imagine with what joy they were hailed if I tell you that some ladies have been reduced to gents dancing pumps.

Poor little Dorothy is still ill, on Sunday it will be 6 weeks since she took ill. We had a letter from Lottie.[53] She says they have had a very hard time and the last news she had from Willie was that he is well – that was on the 11th of September. Good night, Sue.

8 November [1900] I have been feeling so depressed and heart sore these last days that I don't know what to do with myself. Life has lost all its charm for me. I wonder why one can't die when you do not want to live. Only those who love life lose it. God seems so very far away, just as if He has turned his face away from us. Every day the troubles and worries thicken around us and we do not know where to turn for help.

Uncle John[54] has come to the end of what little money he had. If it were not for the few pounds the children earn, they would be destitute. There are hundreds of families in the same case. Dr Messum[55] says he knows of a family who was considered very rich and grand and lived in fine style [but] are [now] so poor that they must live on mealie pap!

Father has such an awful attack of neuralgia in the bones of his head and in his eye that he could not go to school for three days. I am afraid he will have to give it up and then what his wife and child are to live on, I don't know.

Little Dorothy has been dying since Saturday. Oh! the weariness and pain of watching the wee life fade, day by day. Mrs Voss looks worn and thin but has grown even sweeter if that be possible. From last night they [the British authorities] allowed us to be out until 10 [pm]! It seems passing strange to be out after 7 – we hardly know ourselves.

9 November [1900] I had supper at home last night. It was such a curious sensation to be out after 7 o'clock after 5 months imprisonment! We went over to see auntie and the girls and I spent a pleasant evening with them.

Our poor old General Joubert's wife and daughter have been sent out to General Botha to try to persuade him to end this wretched war.[56] I wonder what the result will be? It does seem rather a curious idea.

There have been several marriages between Khakies and Africander women. Of course they move off with their regiments and the women are left to get on as best they may. It just makes us sick to see how the women go on with the soldiers and officers. Nelly Burger's[57] stepdaughter is engaged to one of them. Just imagine that her father is supposed to be fighting and she is engaged to one of the enemy. He is said to be a married man! Some weeks ago Nelly heard that her husband's 10 farms in Vryheid have been burned! Also all their grand furniture which cost hundreds of pounds. Poor girl, she had to pay a price for her loveless marriage! She is only 28 but could pass for 40, she looks so worn.

In a letter Mr Voss received from his daughter Hester, who is at school in Wellington, she tells of a Transvaal boy who had not heard from his home since last October when the war began. Now someone wrote and told him that his father and his two brothers were killed in battle. His mother died of [a] broken heart. The English burned their farm and his two little sisters were so terrified that they fled into the veld and have not been seen since! Is not it awful? Poor boy. Hester says he is half mad with grief.

15 [November 1900] Dorothy has been taken home and the house is desolate. Oh! what a blank such a wee one can leave. She suffered so much. She had dropsy at the last and we had to take turns at carrying her, she could not lie down. Now it is all over and we will carry her no more. She was such a sweet lovely little flower and always had a smile for all. When Sophy came to look at her this morning she said 'Her little life is ended, but she did what she could, she smiled!' Blessed little one, her mission has not been in vain. She has left us with hearts full of longings for better things. I am sure all in this home will be more gentle and loving for Dorothy's sake. And that dear mother of hers! I never saw such a sweet woman in my life. She carries this sorrow so bravely that we can't help weeping for the pain we know she bears so meekly.

20 Nov[ember 1900] It is a rainy afternoon and as I can't go home, I might as well write to you. Everybody seems sure now that the war is to last another year. How many of the poor country people will be left to see the end, I do not know. One thing I do know and that is that we people in Pretoria have no cause to complain of hard times if we compare our lot with theirs. It makes one's heart ache to hear the tales of woe which these poor people tell, who have been brought in by the English. One woman sent her little son to fetch the mules [and] within half an hour the English came and as her husband was still on commando, the farm was burnt down. The woman, in spite of her pleading to wait for her son, was ordered to get into a waggon and go on to Pretoria. To this day she has not heard of the boy.

Another young girl went out for a drive [and] while she was gone the English came, burned the farm and took the family away. Her mother was wild with grief, not knowing what has become of the girl. These are but a few of the many tragic tales we constantly hear. What a wonder that the people hate the English with such bitterness. It is seven months since William left. I am longing to hear from you again.

6 Dec[ember 1900] How the time has gone since I wrote to you last. I left Mrs Voss a week ago. I was so happy with them and it was hard to leave but now that Dorothy is gone, Mrs V can get on. She said a great many nice things about me and shed a few tears when we parted but I reminded her that we still live in the same town and promised to come to her often. I had two other offers but as I am so tired, I decided to come home and rest.

However that is not to be, because one Mr Foote[58] called yesterday and begged me to come to them as his wife is very delicate and needs help badly, so I am going on Monday.

Our food is getting so scarce and there is no meal or flour to be had. We are beginning to dread a famine. The military have of course more than enough, but that won't help us. The people, at least the greater deal, are mad enough to think that some day Oom Paul will come back from Europe with a large army! It is awful that the burghers will not give in – the misery is beyond description.

Pretoria is crowded to its fullest extent with the country people whose farms have all been destroyed. It makes one's heart ache to see the poor things. They only get meat, rice, coffee and flour every 3 days.[59] No milk, sugar or soap. They must cook as best they can. We are often so short of coal that we do not know what to do. Wood we never even see on the market. The poor trees have suffered as much as the people, because we all use the branches and a great many trees have been cut down. If the war lasts another year there will be few trees left.

William Richard Collins in later life. He married Bessie in 1903

16 Dec[ember 1900] Oh! Sue my heart is so full of pain that I feel as if I can't bear it any more. Last night we heard that a man was shot in a fight near Rustenburg and his card was found on him 'Collins of Pretoria'. That is all. If I live to be a hundred I shall never forget the agony it cost me. Oh! Sue, we are almost sure it is our dear boy. Only So, Carlie and I know – Mr vd Merwe told us. We are trying to find out more. It will almost kill auntie and uncle. This suspense is awful, I can't bear it. He was so much to me always.[60]

17 Dec[ember 1900] Just a few lines to tell you our fears are at rest. It is another Collins who was killed and we trust that our dear boy is safe. Ach! child, what I lived through yesterday, no one knows. I longed to fly away somewhere and weep to my heart's content and yet I had just to go about and do my work as if I did not carry a heart as heavy as lead. I am with Mrs Foot.[61] So you can imagine how hard it was to keep up. There were visitors in to tea too. Well, when I got home (I sleep at home) I heard the good news and oh! the relief was beautiful.

PART 3: '... Pretoria belongs to England!'

Yesterday was Dingaan's Day and if you refer to page 4 you will see what it was like last year.[62] Oh! the changes and the sorrow we have lived through.

24 Dec[ember 1900] To think that it is actually Christmas tomorrow, and yet there is war in this unfortunate land. Dear, dear, what weary, weary days we have struggled through. We have grown old and subdued and I, for one, feel as if I have very little love left for life. It will be a sad and dreary day for many. How our poor people in St Helena and Ceylon[63] will long for home and their loved ones.

Poor William, he will be desperately homesick. We will all think of him so much. We are going to have a small gathering at auntie's house and will do our best to make the evening as cheerful as we can. I do wish I could spend the day at home but that is out of the question, as I must cook the [Christmas] dinner here. After all, it is a great thing that Mrs Foote allows me to sleep at home. They are so different to those dear Vosses. Mrs F is so heavy that she wearies one to death. Mr F is just a great careless boy, full of fun and ready to give in to everybody as long as it saves him any worry. Their only child, Harold, is a lovely little fellow of 5 but [is] so spoilt.

Mr WJ Foote, the manager of Payne Bros outfitting store

Now goodbye, dear. I will think of you and wish you all manner of good wishes. Oh!, I wonder if you will ever get this letter? We are rather more hopeful of peace than we were a little while ago.

Yesterday a man called who had surrendered during the week and he told us Kitchener[64] made a speech to all the burghers who are in a camp near town, and told them that he was most anxious for peace. He proposed certain conditions. One was that they should go to their different districts and tell all the burghers who are still fighting just how matters really are, because our poor people hear all sorts of lies about great defeats for the English and so on.[65] We all know that if they could only hear the truth, they would not go on with this awful war.

Wednesday 26 [December 1900] We spent such a bright pleasant evening at auntie's last night. We had a few other friends too and laughed more than we have done the whole of this year. Only we missed William. Oh! I do trust [that by] next Christmas we'll have peace. The heat is almost unbearable. Several babies have died these last few weeks. Our poor little one is very miserable. He has grown so thin and looks quite another baby.

1 January 1901 My hearty wishes for a bright and happy New Year, Sue dear. How I wonder what this new century will bring to us all. Before its close we will all be higher up. Won't it be beautiful? No more pain, no more sorrow, to live forever with our King and oh! to think of having our loved ones, with no fear of parting again. It was our poor William's birthday yesterday and we do not even know whether he is still alive.[66]

14 Jan[uary 1901] I came home last week as Mrs Foote is a good deal better and can get on without help. I was very glad to get home as I am so tired, or lazy, I don't know which. Baby is much better. Poor little chap, he was pretty bad. I daresay by this time you have heard about Kitchener's scheme. Well, we think the terms he offers are wonderfully good and are most anxiously awaiting the result.[67] He sent about 30 men from here. Each man received about 30 proclamations for the burghers. If the people are mad enough to refuse to accept those terms, then there will be nothing for us but just to sit still and see the ruin of this unhappy country and the people.

Our brother Willie was taken prisoner last month. We do not know where he has been sent. It is a relief to know that he is safe.

Lord Kitchener

23 Jan[uary 1901] So the Queen has been taken too.[68] What a glorious reign she had! She was indeed a noble woman. Now she looks at this war with 'larger other eyes', and I wonder what she thinks of it all? We are afraid that when the burghers hear of it they will not surrender because they will be mad enough to think it will cause trouble in England and so they will have more chance.

We are slowly beginning to make up our minds [resign ourselves] to another year of this miserable business. Hundreds and hundreds of women and children were brought in again this week. All the farmers round the town have been ordered in. Poor things, it means ruin to them. They have been working so hard on their lands and now just when everything was coming on well and the fruit ripening, they have to leave it all. On 5th of next month Kitchener will withdraw his terms if the burghers refuse to accept them and he will try other means! We are almost certain that they will refuse to surrender, because they have all gone mad and will not listen to reason. Their one idea now seems to be to cause the English as much trouble and loss as possible, and their helpless women and children must suffer for it. I have lost all patience with our people. When they were fighting in a fair and honourable way and there was still some chance for us it was another thing but now they have as leaders all the worst characters and they are nothing more than highway robbers.

Then the wickedness of going into the Colony again, as if we have not already caused those people enough loss. Oh I am just sick to death of it all, and then they go and pray and declare God will give us the country back!

3 Feb[ruary 1901] I got so many nice things today.[69] Three lovely cakes, a pair of gloves, a pair of shoes, a pretty cake plate, a huge bouquet of flowers and a bottle of sweets, also a lot of fruit! So you see, Sue, in spite of the war, we still have sunshine in between. I thought much about you and wondered whether you were thinking of me. All the other Collinses came and a few other friends and we had coffee and cake in the dining room and enjoyed ourselves in a quiet way.

18 Feb[ruary 1901] Today we heard that Gen L Botha was surrounded [and] that it will be impossible for him to escape. I hope it is true. We are so sad and shocked about the murder of the two peace envoys.[70] It is awful and just shows how utterly demoralised our people have become.

We have had so little rain, we fear a great drought. Last week Helen[71] received a letter from a school friend in which she said that William is safe and says we need not worry about him. You can imagine what a relief it was.

27 October 1901 It seems ages since I wrote the above![72] L Botha has been surrounded and all but captured dozens of times since then and still this war drags on and on and the suffering, sorrow and sin increase by the day. We never hear anything about William, in fact we think we will only meet him in that other country where all will be peaceful and sorrow and death are no more. Child, how weary we are of it all.

We have heard such sad things during this week and our hearts ache for those poor women and helpless little ones. I dare not write in my letters to you about different things, but after this war is over many things which are hidden now will come to light.[73]

Who will ever paint all the misery which the women of this land have endured, who will be able to compensate them for their ruined homes, and for the little ones who are lying in the cemetery by hundreds. Talk of the generosity of the English[74] and the luxury in which the people are kept in the camps! I only wish that the English themselves could have the bitter camp experience for one week, then they would tell less lies and also understand what real suffer[ing] meant. I could tell you such tales of suffering which would make your heart ache for those down-trodden people.

Melrose House, where peace was signed on 31 May 1902

PART 3: '... Pretoria belongs to England!'

1 June 1902 At last, at last we have <u>Peace</u>![75] We did not believe it at first. Oh! I cannot tell you what joy it is to us. To think of all the weary months during which we have hoped against hope for this blessed peace. The news came in at 10 o'clock [22h00] last night. Early this morning some of the people heard it, but as I said we could not believe it. We had been disappointed so often. Now that it is over at last, we wonder how we endured it and trust we will not live to see another war.

Oh! dear, dear to think that it is actually over and oh! to think of all the brave strong men on both sides who have had to give their lives for this cause. There is great joy and rejoicing but I fear there will be far more pain and sorrow in many homes when we begin to get news from our people. We are looking out for William.

Now, Sue, I will close this long letter which is almost three years old. I wonder if you will ever get it, and if it will interest you. I am almost afraid you will weary of it, but at least you will see how often during these long and weary days I have thought of you, who have been so true a friend to me. Of course I have written much, which in calmer moments, would not have been written, but during such times, all are apt to go rather mad. I could send you a copy and leave out what I thought best, but then this letter would not be, as I meant it, an account of our life during the war.

So if you do get it you must not be too critical. Remember it was meant for your eyes alone.

Yours faithfully
BC

Select bibliography

No attempt has been made here to give an exhaustive list of works on the Anglo-Boer War of 1899–1902, nor indeed on Pretoria during the Anglo-Boer War. A selection has instead been made of a few of the more readily available books (and several contemporary works which may be more difficult to find) which illuminate the issues which BC discusses in her letter to Sue.

Allen, V, *Kruger's Pretoria: buildings and personalities of the city in the 19th century*. Cape Town: Balkema, 1971.

Batts, HJ, *Pretoria from within during the war, 1899–1900*. London: John F Shaw, undated.

Dunston, L, *Young Pretoria, 1889–1913*. Pretoria: Heer, 1975.

Grundlingh, AM, *Die 'Hendsoppers' en die 'Joiners': die rasionaal en verskynsel van verraad*. Pretoria: Protea Boekhuis, 1999.

Izedinova, S, *A few months with the Boers: the reminiscences of a Russian nursing sister*. Johannesburg: Perskor, 1977.

Kruger, R, *Goodbye Dolly Gray, the story of the Boer War*. London, 1996.

Longlands Pretoria directory for 1899. Pretoria: State Library reprint, 1979.

Mendelsohn, R, *Sammy Marks: 'The uncrowned king of the Transvaal'*. Cape Town: David Philip, 1991.

Nasson, B, *The South African War 1899–1902*. London: Arnold, 1999.

Pakenham, T, *The Boer War*. London & Johannesburg: Jonathan Ball, 1979.

Pakenham, T, *The Boer War: Illustrated edition*. London & Johannesburg: Jonathan Ball, 1993.

Pretorius, F, *Life on commando during the Anglo-Boer War 1899–1902*. Cape Town: Human & Rousseau, 1999.

Pretorius F, *The Anglo-Boer War, 1899–1902*. Cape Town: Don Nelson, 1985.

Reitz, D, The Denys Reitz trilogy, Emslie, TS (ed), *Adrift on the open veld: the Anglo-Boer War and its aftermath 1899–1943*. Cape Town: Stormberg, 1999.

Scholtz, GD, *Die Tweede Vryheidsoorlog 1899–1902*. Pretoria: Protea Boekhuis, 1998.

Spies, SB, *Methods of barbarism? Roberts and Kitchener and civilians in the Boer republics: January 1900 – May 1902*. Cape Town: Human & Rousseau, 1977.

Spies, SB, *A soldier in South Africa: the experiences of Eustace Abadie 1899–1902*. Johannesburg: Brenthurst Press, 1989.

Spies, SB & Nattrass, G, (eds), *Jan Smuts, memoirs of the Boer War*. Johannesburg: Jonathan Ball, 1994.

Theron, Bridget, *Pretoria at War 1899–1900*. Pretoria: Protea Book House, 2000.

Notes

> **ABBREVIATIONS:**
> TAD – Transvaal Archival Depository, National Archives, Pretoria.
> KAB – Cape Archives, Cape Town.

Introduction

1   BC's diary, 3 February 1901; Death Notice, NAR MHG 47766 (TAD).

2   JH Malan, *Die opkoms van 'n republiek* (Bloemfontein, Nasionale Pers,1929), p 494.

3   Death Notice, NAR MHG 0/9991 (TAD).

4   For biographical information on William Collins senior, see *Dictionary of South African biography*, vol 3, pp 166–167.

5   BC's diary, 26 April, 1900.

6   Private family papers of Advocate William Richard Collins Prinsloo, (Bessie's grandson): Typed list of children of William Collins and Anna Wilhelmina Collins (born Whiskin), signed by JA Collins, their youngest son, dated 3 October 1932.

7   For biographical information on William Whiskin Collins, see *Dictionary of South African biography*, vol 3, pp 167–168.

8   For biographical information on Richard Dixon Collins, John Thomas Collins and James Allison Collins, see Malan, *Die opkoms van 'n republiek*, pp 494–495.

9   BC's diary, 15 March 1900.

10 See letter from MR Haarhoff to GJ Reyneke, Graaff-Reinet, 22 November 1972, reproduced in this introduction, pp 11–12.

11 On the early history of the Ebenhaezer School see City Council of Pretoria, *Pretoria 1855–1955* (Pretoria, Van Schaik, 1955), pp 207–208.

12 BC's diary, 17 June 1900.

13 Death Notice, NAR MHG 0/9991 (TAD).

14   Death Notice, NAR MOOC 3376 (KAB).

15   BC's diary, 9 July 1900.

16   *Dictionary of South African biography*, vol 5, p 145.

17   *Longland's Pretoria directory for 1899* (Pretoria, State Library reprint, 1979), pp 124, 220.

18   BC's diary, see for example entries on 4 March 1900, 6 May 1900 and 3 February 1901.

19   BC's diary, 16 December 1900.

20   For biographical information on William Richard Collins, see *Dictionary of South African biography*, vol 5, p 145.

21   BC's diary, 1 June 1902.

22   Mr GJ Reyneke was the chief archivist of the National Archives at the time.

23   Nelly Meyer, the second wife of General Lucas Meyer, a Boer general, apparently came from Graaff-Reinet. She is mentioned several times in Bessie's letter. See for example 4 March 1900, 9 November 1900 and PART 1, note 95.

24   BC's diary, 27 June 1900.

25   See for example her criticism of the behaviour of some of the Boer women in Pretoria, entry of 28 September 1900.

26   SB Spies (ed), *A soldier in South Africa: the experiences of Eustace Abadie 1899–1902* (Johannesburg, Brenthurst Press, 1989), p 17.

27   Preface by JC Smuts to Deneys Reitz, *Commando*, reprinted in TS Emslie (ed), The Denys Reitz trilogy, *Adrift on the open veld: the Anglo-Boer War and its aftermath 1899–1943* (Cape Town, Stormberg, 1999), p 9.

28   BC's diary, 30 January 1900.

29   BC's diary, 4 March 1900.

30   Thomas Pakenham, *The Boer War* (Johannesburg & London, Jonathan Ball, 1979), p 95.

31   See for example SB Spies & G Nattrass, (eds), *Jan Smuts, memoirs of the Boer War* (Johannesburg, Jonathan Ball, 1994), p 21.

32   Pakenham, *The Boer War*, p xv.

Notes: Part 1

33   Spies & Nattrass (eds), *Jan Smuts, memoirs of the Boer War*, p 39.

34   F Pretorius, *The Anglo-Boer War 1899–1902* (Cape Town, Don Nelson, 1985), pp 57, 81.

35   BC's diary, 20 March, 1900.

36   BC's diary, 6 May 1900.

37   BC's diary, 20 May 1900.

38   BC's diary, 21h30 on 4 June 1900.

39   BC's diary, 28 September 1900.

40   RTJ Lombard, *Ermelo 1880–1980* (City Council, Ermelo, 1980), p 169. See also *Dictionary of South African biography*, vol 5, p 145.

41   Death Notice, NAR MHG 47766 (TAD).

42   Evidence of Elizabeth Bakkes (Bessie's granddaughter).

PART 1
'... these awful days of anxious waiting'

1   Martial law was declared, and its terms published in the *Staats-Courant der ZAR*, the republic's government gazette of the same day, 11 October 1899, the day on which the Anglo-Boer War began.

2   At an Executive Council meeting held on 3 October 1899 it was decided to close all state schools in the ZAR. This made it possible for the school hostel in which the Collins family was living to be converted into a Red Cross Hospital. The adjoining school building, the *Staatsmodelschool*, was used as quarters for captured British officers.

3   The hospital was known as the Bourke Hospital, as the organiser of the project was George Bourke.

4   The Collins family living together in Pretoria at the time comprised the father, Richard Dixon Collins, who had been head of the school hostel and was now appointed to run the Bourke Hospital, his wife Carlie (Carolina Alida, born Hugo) and his two daughters from a previous marriage: Sophy (Martha Sophia) and Bessie (Elizabeth Henrietta Martyn), the author of this letter. See Death Notice, RD Collins, NAR MOOC 3376 (KAB).

5   George Bourke was an eminent Pretoria businessman. He and his brother EF (Eddie) Bourke ran two successful stores: an outfitters in Church Street east and a general merchant store (under George's management) in Church Street west.

6   Miss Frances A Lowrie was the matron.

7   Bremersdorp was a small town in the Cape Colony.

8   General Sir Redvers Henry Buller (1839–1908), Commander-in-Chief of the British forces in South Africa from October to December 1899.

9   The *Staatsmodelschool* or State Model School was a state-run school for boys. It was situated on the north-eastern corner of Van der Walt and Skinner Streets. Prior to the outbreak of the war it had an enrolment of 227 pupils: *Staats-Almanak voor de ZAR, 1899,* p 308.

10 Sophy was Bessie's sister and Carlie was their stepmother.

11 Usually spelt *Landdrost*. An official who had duties similar to those of a magistrate. Pretoria's *Landdrost* at the time was CE Schutte.

12 Presumably for security reasons, as all the Pretoria prisoner-of-war camps were brightly lit by electric lights on tall lampposts. Cornelis Delfos, owner of a local engineering works that specialised in electric lighting plants, was responsible for most of the installation.

13 British soldiers were sometimes nicknamed 'Khakies' because of the khaki-coloured uniform that was issued to each soldier.

14 By the time this entry was written (28 December 1899), the British had suffered a number of significant reverses such as those at Ladysmith (30 October) and Colenso (15 December) on the Natal front, and Stormberg (10 December) and Magersfontein (11 December) on the western front.

15 The pupils who were boarding at the school hostel (*Eerste Staatstehuis*) in which the Collins family lived.

16 Burghers between the ages of 16 and 60 were indeed liable for commando service, but youngsters who were not yet 16 and men far older than 60 were often found at the front: Pretorius, *The Anglo-Boer War* pp 42–43.

17 Presumably BC refers here to the ZAR and the OFS, although the Boer commandos also moved over the republican borders into the British colonies of Natal and the Cape.

18 The correct spelling is Pretorius, a fairly common name in the republics. Other than his surname, his identity is unknown.

NOTES: Part 1

19 JJ van der Merwe was an assistant teacher at the *Staatsmodelschool*. See *Longland's Pretoria directory for 1899*, p 219.

20 According to the letter dated 22 November 1972 from Miss MR Haarhoff to the chief archivist of the National Archives (see Introduction), BC 'married the William she mentions either before or after the war'. There is no indication of William's surname in the diary, nor of Bessie's intention to marry him, but she makes frequent endearing references to him, receives a letter from him 'almost every day' and worries about his safety while he is on commando fighting on the Boer side. He was in fact her first cousin, William Richard Collins. They were married in Pretoria on 21 October 1903: *Dictionary of South African biography*, vol 5, p 145.

21 After suffering defeat at the hands of the Boers at Modderspruit and Nicholson's Nek on 30 October 1899, the British troops under Lieutenant-General White retreated into the Natal town of Ladysmith. The Boer siege of Ladysmith began on 2 November 1899.

22 Lieutenant-General Sir George White was in command of the British troops in Natal. The siege in fact lasted 118 days. White was invalided home soon after the relief of Ladysmith in March 1900: Pakenham, *The Boer War*, pp 366, 370.

23 The Battle of Dundee took place on 20 October 1899. The Boers failed in their objective and there were heavy losses on both sides.

24 At Elandslaagte on 21 October 1899 the Boers were severely trounced and suffered gruesome casualties at the hands of the British lancers. The Hollander Corps, a Pretoria-based volunteer unit, was decimated in this encounter.

25 Michael (Mike) du Toit, whose family were personal friends of the Collinses, was a 2nd lieutenant, Horse Artillery, in the ZAR's State Artillery: *Longland's Pretoria directory for 1899*, p 216.

26 Presumably this refers to the town of Graaff-Reinet in the Cape Colony where Susan Elizabeth Haarhoff (the 'Sue' to whom BC's diary is addressed) was living. It was while the Collins family lived in Graaff-Reinet, where Richard Dixon Collins was a schoolmaster, that Bessie and Sue had become close friends.

27 BC spells *boer* with a lower case b throughout the diary, rather than use the widely accepted *Boer*. This small idiosyncrasy has been retained.

28 Pretorius claims that young boys of 12 and 13 (and sometimes even younger) were frequently found on commando: F Pretorius, *Life on commando during the Anglo-Boer War, 1899–1902* (Cape Town, Human & Rousseau, 1995), pp 237–238.

29 There are a number of sources which describe this particular case of lack of discipline when the Boer commandos occupied Dundee on 23 October 1899. One of the most graphic accounts is that of Deneys Reitz who, as a member of the Pretoria Commando, himself took part in the looting: D Reitz, *Commando*, reprinted in TS Emslie (ed), The Deneys Reitz trilogy, *Adrift on the open veld*, pp 22–23.

30 The allegation that low-class men from Johannesburg were the main culprits appears to be unfounded. Pretorius claims that most of the guilty men were from Bethal, Pretoria and Heidelberg and that 'they came from all classes': Pretorius, *Life on commando*, pp 218–220.

31 See note 24.

32 The German and Dutch volunteer corps.

33 There is certainly some evidence to confirm this rumour, but apparently the commander of the Hollander Corps denied the allegation vigorously: Pretorius, *Life on commando*, p 228.

34 JC Minnaar was the registrar of deeds in Pretoria in 1899: *Longland's Pretoria directory for 1899*, p 153.

35 Hermanus Stephanus Bosman (1848–1933) was a minister of the *Nederduitsch Gereformeerde of Hervormde Kerk* (Dutch Reformed Church) on Church Square from 1876–1926. He was a very influential and well-loved member of Pretoria society: *Dictionary of South African biography*, vol 1, p 104. The Collins family regularly attended his services.

36 Judging from BC's use of capital letters, the beginning of the 20th century was greeted with similar anticipation as the year 2000 and the 'new millennium'. The capitals have therefore been retained.

37 Delivery of letters to and from Pretoria was often irregular during the war, but at no time was the town completely without a postal service. Post to the Cape Colony, where Sue lived, was indeed suspended for a number of months. On 22 July 1900, after the occupation of Pretoria, BC wrote: 'The post is said to be open to the Colony but we receive very few letters.'

38 A Boer encampment. BC spells it 'lager' and this error has been corrected.

39 Colonel (later Major-General) Robert Stephenson Smyth Baden-Powell (1857–1941) was in charge of the British garrison in Mafeking when the town was besieged by the Boers on 13 October 1899. The siege lasted 217 days and was the longest of the war. Mafeking was relieved on 17 May 1900.

40 December-January is the mid-summer season when the temperature climbs very high and 'those poor women' who according to BC lived in cellars, would certainly have been pleased to enjoy the 'fresh air'.

41 A republican national holiday to commemorate the victory by the Voortrekkers (emigrant Boers from the eastern frontier of the Cape Colony, who took part in the Great Trek of 1836–1854) over the Zulu warriors under Dingane on 16 December 1838, on the banks of the Ncome River. The Boers called it the Battle of Blood River and 16 December became known as Dingaan's (or Dingane's) Day.

42 The Dutch Reformed Church on the square.

43 The Battle of Colenso took place on 15 December 1899. The Boers under General Louis Botha achieved a signal victory over the British, who were commanded by General Sir Redvers Buller.

44 The elderly President of the ZAR, Stephanus Johannes Paulus Kruger (1825–1904). He was president from 1883 to 1901 and was fondly known as 'Oom Paul'. 'Oom' (Uncle) is a term of respect in Afrikaans society.

45 This appears to be a reasonably accurate assessment. According to GD Scholtz, *Die Tweede Vryheidsoorlog 1899-1902* (Pretoria, Protea Boekhuis, 1998), p 39, 6 men were killed and 22 wounded. Another source gives the 'total losses' on the Boer side as 38 men: Pretorius, *The Anglo-Boer War*, p 17.

46 Here BC's information is incorrect; the number of casualties she gives is too high. Pretorius (*ibid*, p 17) puts the British casualties at Colenso at 1139, while Spies (ed) in *A soldier in South Africa*, p 54, claims that 'British losses were more than one hundred and forty killed, more than seven hundred wounded and more than two hundred missing or captured.'

47 This rumour was untrue. However, in the light of his irresolution at the Battle of Colenso and the growing demoralisation among the British troops, Buller was replaced as Commander-in-Chief in South Africa by Field Marshal Frederick Sleigh Roberts (1832–1914), who took over from Buller on 10 January 1900. Buller remained in South Africa, however (and suffered further military humiliation, notably at Spionkop on 24 January), before returning to England in October 1900.

48 As part of the emergency regulations introduced during the war, a curfew was imposed in Pretoria. Residents were not permitted to walk or ride in the streets of the town between 6:30 pm (18h30) and 5 am (5h00): *Buitengewone Staats-Courant der ZAR*, 18 November 1899. See also *De Volksstem*, 28 October 1899.

49 Mr and Mrs TG Voss were family friends who lived in Boom Street west. Thomas Voss worked as an inspector in the Department of the Chief Inspector of Offices: *Longland's Pretoria directory for 1899*, pp 174, 216. Bessie later

worked for them in a temporary capacity to help with the housekeeping and the care of Mrs Voss's delicate newborn child.

50   It is not clear which particular encounter BC refers to here. Probably a skirmish at Ladysmith. The unsuccessful Boer offensive at Platrand took place only on the morning of 6 January 1900.

51   Lieutenant-General Sir George White retreated with his force to Ladysmith and the Boer siege of the town began on 2 November 1899. White in fact 'held out' until 28 February 1900. See also notes 21 and 22.

52   The Boer generals came under considerable criticism for their military tactics, particularly the protracted sieges which kept many Boer commandos tied down in virtual inactivity, thus neutralising one of their greatest advantages – their superior mobility compared with the ponderous British force.

53   Again, BC's information is incorrect; it is clear that news filtering through to Pretoria was often inaccurate. Boer commandos under General H Schoeman failed in an attempt to occupy the important Cape Colony railway junctions of Naauwpoort and De Aar, and penetrated only as far as Colesberg. In control of the railway line, the British were able to advance through the Cape unhindered: Pretorius, *The Anglo-Boer War*, p 16.

54   There is evidence that theft was indeed a problem in the Boer commandos. See for example Pretorius, *Life on commando*, pp 224–226.

55   *De Volksstem* (literally: voice of the people) was the only newspaper available in Pretoria during the first (pre-occupation) phase of the war. It was subsidised by the government and inevitably was used as a government propaganda tool. Both Dutch and English editions were available. Despite the fact that it was the butt of much criticism, *De Volksstem* soon became very important to the people of Pretoria because it was one of their very few links with the war front and the world outside.

56   The *Staatsmodelschool* in Van der Walt Street, the prisoner-of-war quarters for British officers.

57   The Bourke Hospital on the south-eastern corner of Van der Walt and Schoeman Streets.

58   Winston Spencer Churchill (later Prime Minister of Britain) was a young war correspondent for the *Morning Post*. On 15 November 1899 he was captured near Chieveley on the Natal front and taken as a prisoner of war to the *Staatsmodelschool* in Pretoria. He escaped on 12 December 1899.

59   Presumably Commandant General Piet Joubert.

60   The British repeatedly shipped reinforcements into South Africa, increasing their overwhelming numerical superiority over the Boer forces.

Notes: Part 1

61   It was Lord Roberts, not Buller, who had lost the use of one eye: *Dictionary of South African biography*, vol 2, p 598.

62   After his defeat at Colenso on 15 December, Buller made a second attempt to break through to Ladysmith. On 16 January he crossed the Tugela and there were a number of skirmishes culminating in the greatest Boer victory of the war: at Spionkop on 24 January 1900. Presumably BC refers here to the skirmishes from 16 January which led to the main battle of 24 January.

63   The entry for 7 January 1900.

64   BC probably refers here to news of the Boer attack on Platrand, south of Ladysmith on the morning of 6 January 1900. The Boer failure was allegedly because of poor leadership and lack of co-operation.

65   William Richard (Willie) was BC's older brother. His wife was Lottie.

66   General Pieter (Piet) Arnoldus Cronjé (1836–1911). BC spells his name Cronje, and this has been corrected. In November 1899 he commanded the Boers on the western front, gaining victories at Modder River (28 November) and Magersfontein (11 December). He surrendered to Roberts at Paardeberg on 27 February 1900. BC's glowing respect for him is largely unwarranted. Although he played a role in the war of 1880–81 and earned great praise for the capture of Jameson's force in 1895–96, his 'virtually undying military fame' became decidedly tarnished in the Anglo-Boer War. He stands accused of being a 'poor strategist', of maintaining slack discipline, of being excessively stubborn, of ignoring good advice and even disobeying orders. His decision to besiege Mafeking has been questioned. He also refused to rid himself of his encumbrances (wagons and burghers' families) which might have made escape from the debacle at Modder River a possibility: *Dictionary of South African biography,* vol 3, pp 185–187. See also PART 1, notes 76 and 84.

67   This excerpt shows clearly that despite her English background, BC was a fiercely staunch Boer supporter. There is no indication in her letters that she changed this stance, although in her typical outspoken manner she was critical of the departure of the senior government officials from Pretoria and the removal of the government funds from the capital just before the British occupation in June 1900.

68   There was a very well-equipped Red Cross hospital in the new *Staatsmeisjesschool* building in Skinner Street. The Hamilton Primary School is presently housed there.

69   Buller's second attempt to relieve Ladysmith culminated in the Battle of Spionkop on 24 January 1900. In this encounter 2000 soldiers under Major-General ERP Woodgate were pinned down by 400 burghers under Prinsloo and Opperman. It was the longest encounter of the war, lasting nine full days. The Boers emerged victorious and prevented the British from relieving the town.

70   Possibly EJB Malherbe, a NZASM railway official: *Longland's Pretoria directory for 1899*, p 150.

71   CFW Jeppe was a draughtsman in the Surveyor General's Department: *Ibid*, p 138.

72   According to Pretorius, *The Anglo-Boer War*, p 17, this was the most serious British reverse of the war. The British had between 2500 and 2700 casualties, while 'Boer losses totalled less than 200'. Another source claims that the British 'had lost fifteen hundred men killed, wounded or captured': Pakenham, *The Boer War*, p 306.

73   See note 69.

74   Here BC refers to the war of 1880–1881 which culminated in a Boer victory over a British force at Majuba on 27 February 1881. This brought the period of British annexation of the Transvaal (1877–1881) to a close and the Boers regained their independence. In older texts the Anglo-Boer War of 1899–1902 is sometimes referred to as the Second War of Independence.

75   Adriaan Jacobus Louw Hofmeyr (1854–1937) was a NG minister and political agitator. He had a reputation for being markedly pro-British and outspoken and was very critical of the government of the ZAR. He was captured by a Boer commando at Palapye in November 1899 and imprisoned in the *Staatsmodelschool* with the British officers: *Dictionary of South African biography*, vol 3, p 401.

76   On the western front, at Paardeberg, near the Modder River in the Orange Free State.

77   Kimberley was relieved on 15 February 1900.

78   Cecil John Rhodes (1853–1902), British imperialist, statesman and financier. He was Prime Minister of the Cape Colony until early 1896, but was discredited and forced to resign when it became clear that he had masterminded the ill-fated Jameson Raid of 1895–96. Boer supporters like BC loathed him because he personified the powerful, avaricious Britain, bent on destroying the ZAR.

79   The Collins family attended the church on Church Square. See also note 35.

80   A national holiday to commemorate the Boer victory over the British on 27 February 1881. See note 74.

81   Dr Jan Willem Boudewijn Gunning (1860–1913) was a medical doctor, teacher of zoology at the *Staatsgymnasium* and director of the State Museum. Opperman's identity could not be traced.

Notes: Part 1

82   Three British officers, Haldane, Le Mesurier and Brockie, escaped from the *Staatsmodelschool* on 27 February 1900.

83   Waterval (BC spells it Waterfal, which has been corrected) was a prisoner-of-war camp 20 km north of Pretoria. British soldiers were imprisoned there, while officers were sent to the *Staatsmodelschool*.

84   Cronjé and about 4000 burghers (not 2000 as BC suggests) were trapped on the north bank of the Modder River. Conditions became progressively more desperate for the Boers and eventually on 27 February 1900, Cronjé surrendered to Lord Roberts.

85   28 February 1900.

86   A koppie (small hill) to the north of Ladysmith, on the Natal front.

87   Presumably BC means Van Reenen's Pass, a pass over the Drakensberg Mountains on the border between the Transvaal and Natal.

88   'Auntie and uncle' were John Thomas Collins and his wife Christina. They lived in Prinsloo Street south. John was the brother of RD Collins (Bessie's father). John's eldest son, William Richard Collins, was therefore BC's first cousin. Bessie and William were married in 1903.

89   Another false rumour.

90   A *Staatsmodelschool* pupil, who lived in the school hostel run by RD Collins.

91   An Afrikaans word meaning 'grandfather'.

92   A Boer victory (11 December 1899) on the western front, near Kimberley in the Cape Colony.

93   There was great speculation on the detrimental effects of the lyddite shells used by the British. They reputedly 'damaged throat and lung tissue' and made the burghers nauseous. The Boers thought that the fumes were poisonous if inhaled and also claimed that they contaminated their food supply. These fears gradually faded as the war progressed: Pretorius, *Life on Commando*, pp 134–135.

94   Balloons were used by the British for reconnaissance purposes. Bullets which expanded on impact (dum-dum bullets) were not widely used and were later withdrawn in compliance with an international ban on their use.

95   General Lucas (Lukas) Johannes Meyer (1846–1902), Boer commander in the war of 1880–81 and the early part of the Anglo-Boer War (notably at Dundee in October 1899). After the occupation of Pretoria in 1900 he took no further part in the war because of declining health. His second wife Nelly

(Nellie) came from Graaff-Reinet, was apparently far younger than her husband and 'was a truly stately woman, one who could have graced any court in Europe': MR Haarhoff – GJ Reyneke, Graaff-Reinet, 22 November 1972.

96 There is no indication of who these people were; possibly family members or friends. Susan Haarhoff did not marry, so they were not her children.

97 The sewing group was initiated by Mrs CE Schutte, wife of the *Landdrost,* in December 1899 and went into operation on 23 January 1900. Pretoria women met at the Palace of Justice building on Church Square. Cloth, thread and buttons were provided by the government.

98 In early March 1900 there were two more confrontations in the Orange Free State near Jacobsdal on the Modder River. On 7 March De Wet's force was defeated at Poplar Grove, and three days later at Abrahamskraal, De la Rey was forced to retreat to avoid being surrounded by the British.

99 Cronjé was certainly the commander of the Boer force on the western front, but it was burghers under De la Rey who took part in the first confrontation at Kraaipan on 12 October 1899, the day after war had been declared. The Boers had destroyed the railway line and when an armoured train sent from Mafeking by Baden-Powell to collect two cannons from Kimberley was derailed, Field-Cornet JC Coetzee fired the first shot of the war as a signal to the burghers to launch the attack: JH Breytenbach, *Die geskiedenis van die Tweede Vryheidsoorlog in Suid-Afrika, 1899–1902* (Pretoria, Staatsdrukker,1969), vol 1, pp 388–389.

100 It is not known to whom BC refers here. The Collins family was a very large one. Bessie's father RD Collins was one of the 12 children of William Collins snr. BC probably also had cousins on her mother's (Viljoen) side of the family.

101 The only Frames listed (p 130) in the *Longland's Pretoria directory for 1899* is WM Frames of Van der Walt Street south.

102 William Richard Collins, the man whom BC later married, was a member of the Lydenburg Commando under Commandant PA Dames: *Dictionary of South African biography*, vol 5, p 145.

103 Roberts met with no opposition when he marched into the Free State capital, Bloemfontein, on 13 March 1900. The Free State government hurriedly moved north to Kroonstad.

104 The Hollanders in the Transvaal were despised by many members of the pro-Boer community. This phenomenon was called '*Hollanderhaat*'. It was alleged that the Kruger government imported Hollanders to senior positions in the civil service rather than appoint South African-born Afrikaners. BC was correct in thinking that the Hollanders would have to find another 'hunting ground';

NOTES: Part 2

the new British military government in Pretoria sent most Dutch officials back to Holland.

105   BC expresses the opinion here that with Pretoria under British control, Cape (and presumably also Natal) people, ie 'colonials' would in future be given preference for public appointments in the Transvaal. To some extent, in the case of the whites, this proved to be true.

106   Pakenham, *The Boer War*, p 340, gives a similar toll: 100 Boers killed and 250 wounded.

PART 2
'The English are advancing ... Oh! the misery of this suspense.'

1   It is unclear exactly who she was, or indeed whether BC meant to write Francis. There are six Francis entries in the *Longland's Pretoria directory for 1899*, p 130.

2   BC's use of the word 'niggers' should not be seen as deliberately racist, but rather as conforming to the attitude held by most white people at the end of the 19th century.

3   Correctly spelt 'kappie'. A hooded bonnet with ties under the chin, traditionally worn by Voortrekker women – presumably to keep the hot African sun off their faces.

4   British soldiers were popularly known as 'Khakies' (see PART 1 note 13) or as 'Tommies'. This latter term was derived from the name 'Tommy Atkins' given to a fictitious British private, typically drawn from the working class: Pretorius, *The Anglo-Boer War 1899–1902*, p 36.

5   James Allison Collins, BC's uncle (the youngest brother of her father Richard Dixon Collins) was Under State Secretary in the OFS government during the war.

6   When Bloemfontein was occupied on 13 March 1900, the seat of the OFS government was moved to Kroonstad.

7   A town in the southern Orange Free State not far from the Orange (Gariep) River.

8   The captured British officers were moved to new, less comfortable quarters called 'The Bird Cage' on the northern side of the Apies River which flows through Pretoria. They were housed in a long shed with a corrugated iron

roof and the camp was surrounded by a high barbed-wire fence. The whole camp was brightly lit at night to minimise the chances of escape.

9   Novels by Charles Dickens.

10   A famous American poet and literary figure. BC was obviously well read, and being the daughter of a schoolmaster, had probably received a good education.

11   BC spells his name incorrectly. Nicolaas Mansvelt (1852–1933), one of Pretoria's leading Hollanders, was the Superintendent of the Education Department and the architect of the education policy in the ZAR.

12   Again BC shows her dislike of the Hollander element in Pretoria, a sentiment shared by many Pretorians. The 'railway system' was the *Nederlandsche Zuid-Afrikaansche Spoorwegmaatschappij* (NZASM) and this Dutch company was directed by another prominent Hollander, GAA Middelberg.

13   The Collins family had moved into the house in 1889 when Richard Dixon Collins was appointed principal of the Ebenhaezer School on the same site. In 1894 this school was closed and the government bought the building to use as a hostel for the boys who attended the *Staatsmodelschool*. Collins stayed on in the house as head of this hostel which became known as the *Eerste Staatstehuis* (First State Hostel).

14   A considerable number of indigent people had come to Pretoria in the late 1890s. Most were from rural districts where the rinderpest (a virulent cattle disease) had reduced many farming communities to abject poverty. A large group arrived in Pretoria from the Colesberg district in the Cape Colony. Many of these families were settled on small erven in the so-called Burgher Right area in the north-western part of town.

15   BC refers to the possible situation after the British occupation of Pretoria. She is apprehensive, it seems, that Pretoria's moral standards will sink to the same level as those in Cape Town. It is not clear what 'sights' she fears will be seen in Pretoria to corrupt the youth.

16   His people (the Boers), his nation, or in the case of his congregation, his 'flock'.

17   A Natal town near the ZAR-Natal border.

18   Mauser rifles were produced by the German manufacturers Fried Krupp Gruson. In May 1896 Commandant General Piet Joubert decided to order 25 000 7 mm Mausers and 10 million cartridges for the ZAR in anticipation of the war. The rifles were delivered in Pretoria in mid-1897: Pretorius, *Life on commando*, pp 80–81. In 1897 another consignment of 12 100 arrived: Breytenbach, *Geskiedenis van die Tweede Vryheidsoorlog*, vol 1, p 84.

Notes: Part 2

19   Lieutenant-General Sir William Forbes Gatacre (1843–1906) was in command on the southern front when the British were defeated by the Boers at Stormberg (10 December 1899). In early April 1900, Roberts decided that Gatacre's tactics in the OFS were below par and he was sent back to Britain: Scholtz, *Die Tweede Vryheidsoorlog*, p 64.

20   BC sees herself as an Afrikaner despite her British background. She was born in Bethulie in the Orange Free State and her Death Notice (NAR MHG 47766, TAD) states that she was a 'Hollands Afrikaner'.

21   On 15 March 1900 Kruger sent a telegram to Botha instructing him to destroy the coal mines and other infrastructure (roads, bridges, etc) on the Natal front before retreating. On 13 May Botha gave the orders that these instructions be carried out. Bridges, culverts, etc, were indeed destroyed but none of the coal mines were damaged. (Thanks to Gilbert Torlage for this latter piece of information). See Breytenbach, *Geskiedenis van die Tweede Vryheidsoorlog*, vol 6, pp 76, 92.

22   BC makes a valid comment here. The morale in the commandos plunged ever lower as the Boer fortunes in the war waned. There were many occasions when burghers simply refused to fight, making excuses to remain in the comparative safety of the laager instead: Pretorius, *Life on commando*, pp 196–197.

23   The 'laagers' or 'refugee camps' BC refers to were early concentration camps. The British authorities transported women and children to such camps, where they were housed under dreadful conditions, resulting in many thousands of deaths before peace was declared in May 1902.

24   Joubert was injured on the Natal front at the end of November 1899 when he fell from his horse. He returned to Pretoria and the Boer military leadership in effect passed to Louis Botha. Joubert died in Pretoria on 27 March 1900 after a short illness.

25   The wife of the Postmaster General, Isaac N van Alphen. Their residence was in Andries Street.

26   The baby was born on 9 April 1900 to Richard and Carlie Collins and was thus BC's stepbrother: Death Notice, Richard Dixon Collins NAR MOOC 3376 (KAB).

27   William was well equipped for the post. He had a legal training and had worked in the State Attorney's office under JC Smuts before the war. After the war and his marriage to Bessie he practised as an attorney in Ermelo in the well-known legal firm, Louw & Collins.

28   Presumably Richard Dixon's mother, Anna Wilhelmina Collins (born Whiskin), the widow of William Collins snr. At the time of Collins snr's

death in 1876 the family farm was in the Ladybrand district. It had been given to him on his retirement by a grateful OFS Volksraad, in recognition of his services to the republic: *Dictionary of South African biography*, vol 3, pp 166–167.

29   At the Begbie ammunition factory in Johannesburg on 24 April 1900. Kruger suspected foul play, and regulations to expel British subjects from the ZAR were stepped up: SB Spies, *Methods of barbarism? Roberts and Kitchener and civilians in the Boer republics: January 1900–May 1902* (Cape Town, Human & Rousseau, 1978), p 20.

30   Possibly the confrontation after De Wet's 16-day siege of Wepener. With the arrival of British reinforcements on 25 April 1900, the Boers were forced to retreat.

31   Towns in the OFS which Roberts took on his way from Bloemfontein (which he left on 3 May 1900) to Kroonstad (which he entered on 12 May 1900) before advancing to Johannesburg and Pretoria.

32   BC is correct here. Boer morale was at a very low ebb. Pretorius claims that 'lack of discipline among the Boer forces was most noticeable at this time': Pretorius, *The Anglo-Boer War*, p 25.

33   The ZAR Volksraad (Legislative Assembly) met for the last session from 7 to 9 May 1900: Bridget Theron, *Pretoria at war 1899–1900* (Pretoria, Protea Book House, 2000), p 233.

34   Bessie Collins and Sue Haarhoff (born 8 May 1871) must thus have been friends for at least 18 years. Bessie was born on 3 February 1873 and at the time of writing (May 1900) would have been 27 years old. They met in Graaff-Reinet where both families lived, and probably became friends in 1882 when Bessie was 9 years old and Sue was 11: Death Notice EHM Collins, NAR MHG 47766 (TAD); MR Haarhoff – GJ Reyneke, Graaff-Reinet, 22 November 1972.

35   The rumours which were circulating in Pretoria were probably about Sarel Eloff's (President Kruger's grandson) daring plan to capture Mafeking (where Baden-Powell was still besieged). The Boer attack on the town on 12 May failed and Mafeking was relieved 5 days later, on 17 May 1900.

36   The British entered Kroonstad on 12 May and the OFS government moved again, this time to Heilbron. It was later obliged to go to Frankfort and then to Bethlehem.

37   Boer women had a reputation for exhorting their men to greater efforts on the war front: Pretorius, *The Anglo-Boer War*, pp 54, 65. In May 1900 Pretoria women held a meeting to discuss ways in which they could help to revive the flagging morale in the commandos. Suggestions were discussed but before

Notes: Part 2

anything could really be accomplished, Pretoria was occupied by the British: Theron, *Pretoria at war,* pp 216–218.

38   Roberts did resort to these tactics, but the policy was only implemented in earnest after the occupation of Pretoria. The first group of Boer women and children left the town on 19 July 1900. They were taken by train to Barberton where the Boers had to take responsibility for their welfare: Spies, *Methods of barbarism?* pp 128–143.

39   A plot to blow up the Johannesburg gold mines in May 1900 was thwarted by the Boer authorities but by October they had altered their stance and decided that this was a justifiable military strategy. Plans that a force of 13 000 Boers would destroy the mines did not, however, materialise: Spies, *Methods of barbarism?* pp 48, 173.

40   There was a rush for seats on all available trains from Pretoria to the safety of Natal and the Cape Colony.

41   This is inaccurate. Kruger was informed of the widespread demoralisation in the commandos and on 2 June 1900 discussions were held in Pretoria on the advisability of surrender. Kruger agreed to consult Steyn of the OFS. It was Steyn who refused to accept the idea of ending the war: Spies & Nattrass, (eds), *Jan Smuts, memoirs of the Boer War,* pp 42–43.

42   A village to the south-east of Pretoria.

43   Volunteers from the Cape Colony (ie British citizens) who joined the Boer commandos. They were commonly known as the Cape rebels.

44   Johannesburg was occupied only on 31 May 1900, two days after BC had made this entry in her letter.

45   General Louis Botha (1862–1919) was in command at the Battle of Colenso when the Boers were victors. He took over as Commandant General of the ZAR after General Joubert's death. In 1907 he became the first Prime Minister of the Transvaal Colony and was later the first Premier of the Union of South Africa.

46   A public meeting was called by the Mayor of Pretoria, PJ Potgieter, on 30 May to form a civilian guard force, but Pretorians were too distraught and tense and the meeting was poorly attended: Theron, *Pretoria at war,* p 237. For a good account of the confusion in Pretoria as the British advanced on the capital see Spies & Nattrass (eds), *Jan Smuts, memoirs of the Boer War,* pp 39–51.

47   Senior members of the government, including President Kruger and State Secretary Reitz in fact left on 29 May to set up a new seat of government in Machadodorp. Schalk Burger and Jan Smuts were left in Pretoria to keep the peace: Spies & Nattrass, (eds) *Jan Smuts, memoirs of the Boer War,* pp 40–41.

48 This was untrue.

49 The national anthem of the ZAR.

50 There was clearly confusion about how close Lord Roberts was to Pretoria. He entered the town only on 5 June, a week after BC had made this entry in her letter.

51 On the removal of the government's gold from Pretoria by JC Smuts, the State Attorney, see Spies & Nattrass, (eds), *Jan Smuts, memoirs of the Boer War*, pp 47–49.

52 Because of the removal of the state funds from the bank, salary cheques were dishonoured when presented. This caused a great deal of anger and criticism of the government. Smuts explains the situation and gives the government's point of view: *Ibid*, pp 48–49.

53 This wild, confused period of looting and disorder is known as the 'chaos and plundering'. For a description of the looting spree and a discussion of the possible reasons behind it, see Theron, *Pretoria at war*, pp 237–241; Spies & Nattrass, (eds), *Jan Smuts, memoirs of the Boer War*, p 42.

54 The steadying hand of authority brought some order to the chaotic situation in Pretoria when Commandant General Louis Botha arrived on the morning of 31 May. He placed the town under military authority and issued a proclamation to halt the plundering and lawlessness.

55 A small river six miles from the centre of Pretoria.

56 See PART 1, note 49. Mr and Mrs TG Voss lived in Boom Street west.

57 A fashionable suburb to the south of the town centre.

58 The Mental Hospital (*Krankzinnigengesticht*) to the south west of Pretoria.

59 The State Hospital, a general hospital at the southern end of Potgieter Street.

60 He was Lieutenant WWR Watson.

61 Here BC clearly means JC Smuts. See notes 51 and 52.

62 There are a number of vivid accounts and some remarkable old photographs of the British entry into Pretoria on 5 June 1900. See for example Theron, *Pretoria at war*, Chapter 8; and a contemporary account, HJ Batts, *Pretoria from within* (London, undated), pp173–178.

PART 3
'... Pretoria belongs to England!'

1. Similar restrictions were imposed in Johannesburg.

2. In both the Orange River Colony and the Transvaal Colony, the British military governments retained the existing laws (including those affecting Africans) after occupation. Black people had high hopes that the British authorities would ensure that they were more fairly treated but their hopes were soon dashed. Some minor concessions were subsequently made to African and Indian people. See Spies, *Methods of barbarism?* pp 67–68.

3. BC's attitude towards people of colour can only, in retrospect, be described as racist. This was the prevailing attitude of the time among most white South Africans. The evidence in her letters suggests that she was also biased against Hollanders.

4. After the occupation of Pretoria there were only two more confrontations which could be described as set-piece battles: those at Diamond Hill (11–12 June) and Dalmanutha (25 August). Thereafter the Boer leaders decided to dispense with cumbersome wagontrains and trench warfare and to make the best possible use of their main asset: their superior mobility. They turned to guerrilla warfare.

5. General John Denton Pinkstone French (1852–1925), British commander who, as the leader of the cavalry division, was prominent in the relief of Kimberley. He was later in command in the Cape Colony.

6. BC was employed by the Vosses (from early June to 30 November 1900) to help with the children and the housekeeping when Mrs Voss gave birth to her baby girl.

7. BC spells this name Kathie and Cathie interchangeably. This has been retained as it is not clear which of the two is correct.

8. The Voss home in Boom Street was between Market (now Paul Kruger) and Koch Streets, admittedly a long walk for Bessie from the Collins residence! She would have had to walk 7 street blocks to the north, turn left and walk westwards for a further 2½ blocks.

9. BC's young stepbrother, Richard Hugo. He was nicknamed Buller after the British general.

10. The Bourke Hospital (where the Collins family still lived) and the *Staatsmodelschool* adjoining it. Before the occupation of Pretoria the school had been used as prisoner-of-war quarters for the British officers.

11 The report BC heard was exaggerated. Less than 30 British men were killed and 100 wounded. The Battle of Diamond Hill or Donkerhoek (11–12 June 1900) in fact ended with the retreat of Botha's burghers, but they had fought bravely and had gained new hope.

12 Buller was advancing from Natal at the time with 20 000 men. He was to link up with the main British force in the Transvaal in July 1900. The 'plague' was probably typhoid, a disease that was very prevalent in many of the British camps: Pakenham, *The Boer War*, p 422.

13 It is unclear who Helen was. She is also mentioned in the entry of 22 September 1900 and 18 February 1901. In this latter entry it appears that Helen may perhaps be BC's cousin, William Richard's sister. See PART 3, note 71.

14 Roberts had come under considerable criticism for the inadequate administrative arrangements in British field hospitals in South Africa. Pakenham calls it Roberts's 'hospital scandal' and claims that 'nothing better illustrates Roberts's limitations as a military commander than the fact that … his field medical services were in as scandalous a state as the fixed hospitals at Bloemfontein', where conditions were appalling. The number of deaths from diseases such as typhoid, for example, had increased alarmingly by 1900: Pakenham, *The Boer War*, p 422. See also note 12.

15 For background on British military administration of the ZAR see Spies, *Methods of barbarism?* pp 67–70.

16 In typical Victorian style, BC uses a polite euphemism: Mrs Voss's 'little affair' was the birth of her baby.

17 Herman Dirk van Broekhuizen acted in Revd Bosman's place in the Pretoria NG church on the square during the war. He later served in the scouting corps under Danie Theron, and was captured and exiled because he refused to take the oath of neutrality demanded by the British. He returned to South Africa in 1903: *Dictionary of South African biography*, vol 4, p 676.

18 The British issued several proclamations in the two republics to the effect that burghers who had laid down their arms and were prepared to take an oath to 'abstain from further participation in the war' could return to their homes: Spies, *Methods of barbarism?* p 34–35.

19 A porridge made from maize meal.

20 BC does not generally use this term (she tends to use the word 'niggers' instead, except when she quotes someone else) for black people, but it was the common usage of the day, and does not necessarily denote racism. See for example JC Smuts's use of this term and the footnote by the editors of his memoirs: Spies & Nattrass (eds), *Jan Smuts, memoirs of the Boer War*, p 50, and note 27 on p 201. See also BC's entry of 6 October 1900.

Notes: Part 3

21 According to Spies, Roberts gave permission for the publication of this newspaper in Pretoria 'under military auspices' to counteract the 'false and malicious' reports spread by *De Volksstem*. The first number appeared on 26 June 1900, but the *Pretoria Friend* ceased publication after 14 July 1900: Spies, *Methods of barbarism?* pp 84–85.

22 Efforts to trace the whereabouts of this new Pretoria home have been unsuccessful. Richard Collins must have moved out of Pretoria soon after the war. Bessie married in 1903 and moved with her husband to Ermelo. A directory of 1913 indicates that Richard Dixon no longer lived in Pretoria. He died in Wellington in the Cape on 16 October 1920: Death Notice, NAR MOOC 3376 (KAB).

23 It is not clear why RD Collins was given a rent free house. He was possibly continuing the post with the Red Cross as manager/secretary of the Bourke Hospital although there was no longer accommodation for him and his family there. Perhaps the rent free home was in lieu of a salary. He was later asked to help run a small school for 40 pupils. See entries of 5 October, 22 October and 8 November 1900.

24 BC's mother, Margaretha Louisa (born Viljoen), of whom Bessie speaks so lovingly in a later entry, and of whom she no doubt had happy memories, died in the house on 3 June 1895: Death Notice, NAR MHG 0991 (TAD).

25 Odette Gardhuizen. See PART 2, 23 April 1900.

26 Bessie's statement is correct. See for example Spies, *Methods of barbarism?* p 158.

27 Hans Cordua was a 23-year-old German living in the ZAR. The British authorities claimed that he was the instigator of a plot to kidnap Roberts and hand him over to the Boers. The chief witness at Cordua's trial was a Spaniard called Gano, whom Cordua claimed had 'inveigled him into the plot' by plying him with alcohol and giving him false information. Evidence was also led that Cordua was 'eccentric' and 'weak-minded'. In a trial lasting from 16–21 August 1900, Cordua was found guilty and sentenced to death. He was shot by a firing squad on 24 August. See Spies, *Methods of barbarism?* pp 71, 161–162.

28 This is incorrect. He was a German.

29 BC spells this name incorrectly (Garno instead of Gano). This error has been rectified.

30 Major PE Erasmus was second in command at the State Artillery: *Longland's Pretoria directory for 1899*, p 216.

31 The British established five prisoner-of-war camps in Ceylon (Sri Lanka), the largest being Diyatalawa which housed 5000 Boer prisoners: Pretorius, *The Anglo-Boer War*, p 50.

32 Mr and Mrs Melt van der Spuy were neighbours to the Voss family. There was a vacant stand between their two houses. Melt van der Spuy was the Secretary of the Board of Examiners: *Longland's Pretoria directory for 1899*, pp 23, 168.

33 Presumably because Pretoria residents were under surveillance by the British authorities.

34 General Christiaan Rudolph de Wet (1854–1922) was one of the most outstanding Anglo-Boer War generals. Once the Boer strategy had changed from set battle tactics to guerrilla warfare with the emphasis on mobility, he came into his own and became a continual harassment to the British, damaging communications, launching lightning attacks on their convoys, and always eluding their strenuous efforts to catch up with him. BC is correct when she says that even the British were in awe of his elusiveness.

35 While in the Lydenburg area of the Transvaal, Botha had contracted a throat infection and had to recuperate for a few days at Hectorspruit. By 24 September he was well enough to move his troops to the north: *Dictionary of South African biography*, vol 4, p 44.

36 Vivian, the 6-year-old son of Mrs and Mrs Voss. See entry of 12 June 1900.

37 The baby girl born to Mrs Voss in early July. See entry of 9 July 1900.

38 Margaretha Louisa Collins (born Viljoen) who had died in Pretoria 5 years previously on 3 June 1895: Death Notice, NAR MHG 0/9991 (TAD).

39 At this point BC has crossed out nine full lines of her letter. What she had written (the handwriting is definitely hers) was very effectively blanked out with the same pen. All efforts to read the gist of what had been written here have proved fruitless. Judging from the information immediately preceding the erased section, one can only speculate that perhaps she had written something about Carlie, her father's second wife, had thought better of giving Sue the information, and then had obliterated the lines. BC's final sentence of the 26 September entry is probably significant. She wrote: 'We are not needed in our home any more'. She does not provide Sue with any explanation for having blanked out the nine lines.

40 BC obviously has a very strict, Victorian code of morals insofar as the behaviour of well-bred women is concerned. Added to this she is very outspoken – perhaps more so to Sue than she would ordinarily have been.

Notes: Part 3

(See for example her remarks made on 1 June 1902 as she closes the letter.) In his exhaustive account of civilians in the Anglo-Boer War, Spies, *Methods of barbarism?* makes no mention of Boer women in Pretoria behaving in an untoward manner to British soldiers or officers.

41 Annie Frances Bland Botha, born Emmett (1864–1937) was Commandant General Louis Botha's wife. She stayed on in her Pretoria home after the British occupation. She had an impeccable reputation and was highly regarded by both Boer and British leaders. Soon after the fall of Pretoria she visited her husband outside the capital and then met Roberts on her return, the intention being for her to be an intermediary in discussions about peace. In February 1901 she went to Ermelo to see her husband and discussions between Kitchener and Botha were arranged several weeks later. Perhaps this contact with senior British officers was misconstrued by BC: Spies, *Methods of barbarism?* pp 91–91, 208–209.

42 Farm burning was one of the British tactics which eventually brought the Boers to their knees. The scorched earth policy, ie burning Boer homesteads and thus destroying their possible support base, was started early as February 1900 under Roberts, but was stepped up when Kitchener took over supreme command on 29 November 1900.

43 Presumably in Burgers Park, bounded by Van der Walt, Visagie, Andries and Jacob Maré Streets.

44 Vivian Voss had contracted scarlet fever, so it seems likely that baby Dorothy had caught this from her brother despite attempts to keep her from possible infection: See entries of 22 and 23 September 1900.

45 Presumably someone employed to assist with the domestic chores in the Voss household.

46 See note 20 of PART 3.

47 Kruger crossed the ZAR border on 11 September 1900 en route to Delagoa Bay where he was to sail for Europe. He boarded a Dutch ship only on 19 October 1900, so on his birthday of 1900, the day on which BC wrote this, he was still in Lourenço Marques: *Dictionary of South African biography*, vol 1, p 453.

48 William was a *bittereinder*, a burgher who refused to lay down arms. He fought on to the 'bitter end'.

49 All three of these Pretoria women were prominent in various charitable organisations, helping in the hospitals and with the distribution of food to indigent Boer families.

50 It is not clear where or exactly when this school was opened. A number of makeshift schools were started in Pretoria during the war, but all state schools

were closed by the ZAR government in October 1899 when war appeared to be imminent: Theron, *Pretoria at war,* pp 73–74.

51 BC's opinion of the guerrilla tactics adopted by the Boers after July/August 1900! The rumours of 'great battles' in which the Boers were victorious were unfounded.

52 Prince Christian Victor, a soldier grandson of Queen Victoria, died of typhoid in Pretoria and was buried in the local graveyard.

53 Lottie was BC's sister-in-law, married to Willie.

54 John Thomas Collins, Richard Dixon Collins's brother. John was the father of William Richard Collins, the man Bessie later married.

55 Dr GB Messum, the District Surgeon.

56 Mrs Hendrina Joubert and her daughter left Pretoria on 5 November 1900 with a letter for Botha from local industrialist and entrepreneur, Sammy Marks. Marks appealed to Botha to use his influence with the other leaders to persuade them that it was 'hopeless to continue the struggle': Spies, *Methods of barbarism?* p 99.

57 General Lucas Meyer's second wife. See also PART 1, note 95.

58 WJ Foote was the manager of Payne Brothers of Church Street, an outfitting store. The family lived in Arcadia in Church Street east.

59 On British strategies for dealing with the women and children who flocked into the towns when the policy of farm burning was accelerated, see Spies, *Methods of barbarism?* pp 143–153.

60 BC's anguish is so intense that 'our dear boy' was presumably William Richard Collins, her first cousin and the man she was later to marry.

61 BC is inconsistent in the spelling of the name 'Foote'. She spells it here without the e. The available sources are not much help. In *Longlands Pretoria directory for 1899*, p 130 it is given as 'Foot', while in Lola Dunston, *Young Pretoria, 1889–1913* (Pretoria, Heer, 1975) p 114, the name is spelled 'Foote'.

62 See PART 1, entry for 3 January 1900, p 28.

63 Some of the Boer prisoners of war were taken to St Helena and Ceylon (Sri Lanka).

64 Field Marshal Earl Herbert Horatio Kitchener (1850–1916) came to South Africa as Chief of Staff to Lord Roberts in January 1900. He succeeded Roberts as Commander-in-Chief on 29 November 1900 and it was Kitchener who intensified the twin policies of farm burning and concentration camps

Notes: Part 3

(initiated in part by Roberts) which finally brought the Boers to such desperation that they gave up the struggle.

65 For details of Kitchener's address to surrendered burghers at the Pretoria 'Rest Camp' on 21 December and his proclamation of 20 December 1900, offering the burghers favourable terms if they agreed to lay down their arms, see Spies, *Methods of barbarism?* pp 180-183, 202.

66 'Our poor William' was still very much alive. William Richard Collins was born on 31 December 1876 and died on 28 February 1944 at the age of 67 years: *Dictionary of South African biography*, vol 5, p 145.

67 Kitchener's 'scheme', was to allow burghers to return to their families if they agreed to lay down their arms and sign an oath of neutrality. At the same time he began to enforce the farm burning and concentration camp system which led to untold suffering and the deaths of thousands of women and children of all races. In his *Methods of barbarism?* p 185, Spies claims that the British argument that the system was 'the only humane alternative' has flaws. He points out that the majority of the inmates had not gone into the camps voluntarily, and that certain categories of inmates were singled out for preferential treatment. It would certainly seem that the concentration camps were established for military rather than humane reasons.

68 Queen Victoria died on the Isle of Wight on 22 January 1901 after a reign of 63 years.

69 BC, Elizabeth Henrietta Martyn (Bessie) Collins was born on 3 February 1873 in Bethulie in the Orange Free State, where her father had opened the town's first school. In 1879 the family moved to Graaff-Reinet in the Cape Colony, where Bessie became close friends with Sue (Susan Elizabeth Haarhoff): Death Notice, NAR MHG 47766 (TAD); Malan, *Die opkoms van 'n republiek*, p 493.

70 Only one of the two peace emissaries (Johannes Jacobus Morgendaal) died, and it is open to question whether he was murdered. For an account of the incident see Spies, *Methods of barbarism?* pp 203-204.

71 From the evidence of this entry, Helen may possibly be William Richard's sister. One of Bessie and William's children (their eldest daughter, born 13 June 1908) was named Helene, which would strengthen this supposition. See also PART 3, note 13.

72 It was in fact more than 8 months, the longest gap in BC's letter to Sue. Following this, a little more than 7 months was to elapse before she made the next (final) entry on 1 June 1902. BC gives no reason for the comparatively infrequent entries in the last 15 months of the war.

73 BC has apparently heard by this time of the horrors of the concentration camps and the spiralling number of women and children who have died in these camps. See also PART 3, notes 64, 65 and 67.

74 Whereas BC was previously inclined to regard 'Kitchener's terms' in a favourable light (see entries on 24 December 1900 and 23 January 1901), she is now thoroughly disillusioned.

75 On 31 May 1902 the Vereeniging Peace Agreement was signed at Melrose House in Jacob Maré Street in Pretoria. BC's relief that the war had finally ended is echoed in the words of Pakenham, *The Boer War*, p 571: 'But whatever it was, and whatever it was for, it was over.'

Index

Abrahamskraal, Battle of 88 n. 98
Accession to National Archives 12
Africans 18, 19, 43, 55, 64–65, 95 n. 2, 96 n. 20
Africans, attitude of (at occupation) 55, 95 n. 2
Age of burghers, *See* Call-up, age liable for
Amajuba Day 34, 36, 86 n. 80
Andries Street 91 n. 25, 99 n. 43
Anglo-Boer War, causes of 16–17
   outbreak of 10, 11, 13, 17, 80 n. 9
   phases of 14, 17–18 *See also* Peace
Apies River 89 n. 8
Arcadia 100 n. 58
Armstrong, Mrs H 65, 99 n. 49
Arnoldi, Mrs M (Marie) 7

Baden-Powell, General RSS 15, 28, 28 (photo), 82 n. 39, 88 n. 99, 92 n. 35
Bakkes, Mrs Elizabeth (Liz) 7, 79 n. 42
Balloons, 37, 87 n. 94
Barberton 93 n. 38
Begbie Factory, explosion at 47, 92 n. 29
Bethal Commando 82 n. 30
Bethlehem 92 n. 36
Bethulie 9, 10, 42, 43, 91 n. 20, 101 n. 69
'Bird Cage' 42, 89–90 n. 8
Bittereinders (Bitter-enders) 11, 99 n. 48
Blacks, *See* Africans
'Black Week' 17
Bloemfontein 10, 11, 17, 18, 21, 38, 40, 41, 57, 88 n. 103, 89 n. 6, 92 n. 31, 96 n. 14
Blood River, Battle of, *See* Ncome River, Battle of
Boom Street 95 n. 8
Booyens, JJ ('Oupa') 37
Boshof, President JN 9
Bosman, Anna 64
Bosman, Revd HS 27, 28, 34, 43–44, 45, 46, 49, 63–64, 82 n. 35, 96 n. 17
Bosman, Mrs HS 64
Botha, General (later Commandant General) L (Louis) 18, 20, 51, 51 (photo), 62, 66, 68, 73, 91 n. 21, 91 n. 24, 93 n. 45, 94 n. 54, 96 n. 11, 98 n. 35, 99 n. 41, 100 n. 56
Botha, Mrs L (Annie) 20, 63, 99 n. 41
Bourke, EF (Eddie) 80 n. 5
Bourke, GM (George) 22, 22 (photo), 80 n. 3–5
Bourke Hospital 21 (photo), 21–23, 23 (photo), 30, 31, 33, 35, 56, 59, 79 n. 2–4, 84 n. 57, 95 n. 10, 97 n. 23

Bremersdorp 22, 80 n. 7
British, criticism of 29, 32, 65, 74
British military administration 96 n. 15
British numerical superiority, *See* Numerical superiority of British
British officers in State Model School 22–23, 23 (photo), 29–30, 34, 39, 79 n. 2, 84 n. 56, 84 n. 58, 86 n. 75, 87 n. 83
British officers, moved to new quarters 42, 43, 89–90 n. 8
Brockie, Officer 34, 87 n. 82
Buller, General Sir RH 22, 29, 31, 56, 80 n. 8, 83 n. 47, 85 n. 61, 85 n. 62, 85 n. 69, 96 n. 12
'Buller', *See* Collins, Richard Hugo
Burger, General SW (Schalk) 93 n. 47
Burgers Park 64, 99 n. 43
Burgher Right erven 90 n. 14
Burials 31, 33, 46, 67

Call-up, age liable for 23, 25, 47–48, 80 n. 16, 81 n. 28
Cape Colony 21, 59, 64, 73, 80 n. 17, 82 n. 37, 83 n. 41, 84 n. 53, 86 n. 78, 87 n. 92, 89 n. 105, 90 n. 14, 93 n. 40, 93 n. 43, 95 n. 5, 101 n. 69
Cape railway line 84 n. 53
Cape rebels 50, 51, 93 n. 43
Cape Town 9, 22, 37, 41, 43, 90 n. 15
Century, new twentieth 27, 72
Ceylon (Sri Lanka) 61, 71, 98 n. 31, 100 n. 63
Chamberlain, Sir Joseph 16
Chaos and plundering, *See* Looting
Chieveley 84 n. 58
Christian Victor, Prince 67, 100 n. 52
Christmas Day 30, 71
Church, Dutch Reformed (*Nederduitsch Gereformeerde of Hervormde Kerk*) 28, 34, 46, 82 n. 35, 83 n. 42, 86 n. 75, 86 n. 79, 96 n. 17
Churchill, WS 31, 84 n. 58
Church Square 47–48, 54 (sketch), 82 n. 35, 86 n. 79, 88 n. 97, 96 n. 17
Church Street 80 n. 5, 100 n. 58
Coal mines, destruction of 45, 91 n. 21
Coetzee 24
Coetzee, Field-Cornet JC 88 n. 99
Colenso, Battle of 28–31, 34–35, 80 n. 14, 83 n. 43 and 45–47, 85 n. 62, 93 n. 45
Colesberg 29, 84 n. 53, 90 n. 14
Collins, Miss (later Mrs WR) EHM (Elizabeth Henrietta Martyn, 'BC', Bessie) title page photo, 6–7, 9–14, 17–20, 32, 34, 44, 56, 67, 70, 73, 77 n.1, 79 n. 4, 80 n. 10, 83–84 n. 49, 85 n. 67, 86 n. 78, 87 n. 88, 90 n. 10, 91 n. 26, 95 n. 3, 95 n. 6–10, 97 n. 24, 100 n. 60, 101 n. 69, 101 n. 71
    attitude to people of colour 12, 40, 41, 55, 58, 64–65, 95 n. 3, 96 n. 20
    birth of 9, 73, 91 n. 20, 92 n. 34, 101 n. 69
    character of 6, 11–12, 20, 85 n. 67, 98 n. 40
    death of 7, 20
    friendship with Sue 6, 10, 49, 75, 81 n. 26, 92 n. 34, 101 n. 69

INDEX

    home of, 10–11, 21 (photo), 21–22, 23 (photo), 43, 59, 71, 79 n. 2, 90 n. 13, 97 n. 22, 97 n. 24
    letters, description of 12–15, 18, 101 n. 72
    marriage to William Richard Collins 11, 12, 20, 70, 81 n. 20, 87 n. 88, 88 n. 102, 91 n. 27, 97 n. 22, 100 n. 54, 100 n. 60
Collins, Miss Helen 11, 57, 62, 68, 73, 96 n. 13, 101 n. 71
Collins, Helene 101 n. 71
Collins, JA (James Allison, 'Uncle Jim') 10, 42, 77 n. 6, 77 n. 8, 89 n. 5
Collins, JH (John Henry) 11
Collins, JT (John Thomas) 10, 11, 37, 48, 67, 70, 77 n. 8, 87 n. 88, 100 n. 54
Collins, Mrs JT (Christina, born Olivier) 11, 37, 45–46, 48, 68, 70–71, 87 n. 88
Collins, Miss MS (Martha Sophia, 'Sophy', 'So') 11, 22, 29–30, 32, 34, 44, 47, 49, 58, 62–64, 69, 70, 79 n. 4, 80 n. 10
Collins, RD (Richard Dixon) 9–13, 22, 42, 43 (photo), 47, 49, 51, 57, 59, 62, 64, 66, 68, 77 n. 8, 79 n. 4, 81 n. 26, 87 n. 88, 88 n. 100, 89 n. 5, 90 n. 13, 91 n. 26, 91 n. 28, 97 n. 22–23, 99 n. 50, 100 n. 54, 101 n. 69
Collins, Mrs RD (Carolina Alida, 'Carlie', born Hugo) 11, 22, 37, 43 (photo), 47, 49, 59, 70, 79 n. 4, 80 n. 10, 91 n. 26, 98 n. 39
Collins, Mrs RD (Margaretha Louisa, born Viljoen) 9, 11, 63, 66, 77 n. 3, 88 n. 100, 97 n. 24, 98 n. 38–39
Collins, RH (Richard Hugo, 'Buller') 47–49, 56–57, 59, 71–72, 91 n. 26, 95 n. 9
Collins, William (snr) 9–10, 77 n. 4, 77 n. 6, 88 n. 100, 91–92 n. 28
Collins, Mrs William snr (Anna Wilhelmina, born Whisken) 9–10, 47, 77 n. 6, 91 n. 28
Collins, WR (William Richard) (later Colonel, later Minister) 7, 11–12, 20, 24, 28–31, 36, 38–39, 41, 47, 50, 56–57, 59, 64–66, 69–70, 70 (photo), 71–73, 75, 78 n. 20, 81 n. 20, 87 n. 88, 88 n. 102, 91 n. 27, 96 n. 13, 99 n. 48, 100 n. 54, 100 n. 60, 101 n. 66, 101 n. 71
Collins, WR (Willie) 9, 11, 32, 40, 42–43, 47–48, 50, 56, 67, 72, 85 n. 65, 100 n. 53
Collins, Mrs WR (Lottie) 32, 43, 47, 67, 85 n. 65, 100 n. 53
Collins, WW (William Whisken) 9–10, 77 n. 7
Concentration camps 18–19, 45, 49, 74, 91 n. 23, 93 n. 38, 100 n. 60, 101 n. 67, 102 n. 73
Cordua, Hans 20, 60 (photo), 60–61, 97 n. 27
Cronjé, General PA (Piet) 13, 19, 20, 32, 33, 35, 35 (photo), 36–39, 39 (photo), 40–41, 44, 85 n. 66, 87 n. 84, 88 n. 99
Cronjé, Mrs PA 39, 39 (photo), 41
Curfews 6, 29, 55, 58, 68, 83 n. 48

Dalmanutha, Battle of 95 n. 4
Dames, Commandant PA 11, 88 n. 102
De Aar 84 n. 53
Delagoa Bay 99 n. 47
De la Rey, General JH (Koos) 88 n. 98–99
Delfos, Cornelis 80 n. 12
Demoralisation of Boer forces 6, 14, 17–18, 45, 48–49, 73, 91 n. 22, 92 n. 32, 92–93 n. 37, 93 n. 41
Departure of officials, *See* Government officials leave Pretoria
De Volksstem 20, 30, 38, 83 n. 48, 84 n. 55, 97 n. 21

De Wet, General CR (Christiaan) 18, 62, 62 (photo), 65–66, 88 n. 98, 92 n. 30, 98 n. 34
Diamond Hill (Donkerhoek), Battle of 95 n. 4, 96 n. 11
Dickens, Charles 42
Dingaan's Day 28, 71, 83 n. 41
Diyatalawa Camp 98 n. 31
Dum-dum bullets 37–38, 87 n. 94
Dundee 24–27, 30, 81 n. 23, 82 n. 29, 87 n. 95
Du Plessis 31
Durban 66
Dutch Reformed Church, *See* Church, Dutch Reformed
Du Toit, Lieutenant M (Mike) 24–27, 25 (photo), 44, 81 n. 25
Du Toit, Mrs M (Katie) 25, 26
Du Toit, Miss 24, 26, 53

Ebenhaezer School 10, 90 n. 13
Elandslaagte, Battle of 24, 27, 32, 81 n. 24
Eloff, Sarel 92 n. 35
Erasmus, Major PE 60–61, 97 n. 30
Erasmus, Mrs PE 61
Ermelo 7, 20, 91 n. 27, 97 n. 22, 99 n. 41
Europe 70, 99 n. 47

Farm burning, *See* Scorched earth policy
First War of Independence (First Anglo-Boer War) 33, 39, 86 n. 74, 87 n. 95
Foote, WJ 69, 71, 71 (photo), 100 n. 58
Foote, Mrs WJ, 69–72, 100 n. 58
Foote, Harold 71
Fourteen Streams 47, 92 n. 31
Frames, Norman 39
Frames, WM 39, 88 n. 101
Frances, Annie 41
Frankfort 92 n. 36
French, General JDP 55–56, 95 n. 5
Fried Krupp Gruson 90 n. 18
Funds, state, withdrawn from National Bank, *See* State funds removed from Pretoria

Gano 60, 97 n. 27
Gardens as source of food 29, 38
Gardhuizen, Miss Odette 47, 59, 62–63, 97 n. 25
Gatacre, Lieutenant-General Sir WF 44, 91 n. 19
German Corps 27, 82 n. 32
Germany 16
Girls' School (*Staatsmeisjesschool*) Hospital 32, 85 n. 68
Gold mines, plans to destroy 49, 93 n. 39
Government Gazette (of British military government) 55, 58

INDEX

Government Gazette (Staats-Courant) 79 n. 1, 83 n. 48
Government officials leave Pretoria 6, 20, 51–53, 85 n. 67, 93 n. 47
Graaff-Reinet 6, 10, 12, 24, 78 n. 23, 81 n. 26, 87–88 n. 95, 92 n. 34, 101 n. 69
Great Trek 83 n. 41
Guard force, formation of 51, 93 n. 46
Guerrilla tactics of Boers 14, 18, 66, 95 n. 4, 98 n. 34, 100 n. 51
Gunning, Dr JWB 34, 86 n. 81

Haarhoff, Cecil 13
Haarhoff, Miss MR 12–13, 81 n. 20, 88 n. 95, 92 n. 34
Haarhoff, Miss SE (Susan Elizabeth, 'Sue') 6, 10, 12, 49, 75, 81 n. 26, 88 n. 96, 92 n. 34, 101 n. 69
Haldane, Officer 34, 87 n. 82
Hamilton Primary School 85 n. 68
Hectorspruit 98 n. 35
Heidelberg Commando 82 n. 30
Heilbron 92 n. 36
Hofmeyr, Revd AJL 15, 33, 86 n. 75
Hollander Corps 27, 81 n. 24, 82 n. 32–33
Hollanders 19, 27, 40, 43, 45, 49, 50, 59, 88–89 n. 104, 90 n. 11–12
Honey, Mrs EG 65, 99 n. 49
Hospital, *See* Bourke Hospital, Girls' School Hospital, Mental Hospital, Volks Hospital
Hostel (of State Model School, First Hostel, *Eerste Staatstehuis*) 10–11, 21, 21 (photo), 23 (photo), 79 n. 2, 79 n. 4, 80 n. 15, 90 n. 13
Hunt, Colonel 30

Illustrated London News 54 (sketch)
Indians 40, 95 n. 2
Irene 49, 93 n. 42

Jacob Maré Street 99 n. 43, 102 n. 75
Jacobsdal 38, 88 n. 98
Jameson Raid 85 n. 66, 86 n. 78
Jeppe, CFW 33, 86 n. 71
Johannesburg 17, 26, 47–49, 51–52, 56, 58, 92 n. 29, 92 n. 31, 93 n. 39, 93 n. 44, 95 n. 1
Johannesburg Commando 82 n. 30
Joubert, Commandant General PJ (Piet) 31, 45–46, 46 (photo), 65, 68, 84 n. 59, 90 n. 18, 91 n. 24, 93 n. 45
Joubert, Mrs PJ (Hendrina) 46, 68, 100 n. 56

'Khakies' (British soldiers) 58, 63, 80 n.13, 89 n. 4, *See also* 'Tommies'
Kimberley 16, 17, 33, 86 n. 77, 87 n. 92, 88 n. 99, 95 n. 5
Kitchener, General (later Field Marshal, Earl) HH 18, 71–72, 72 (photo), 99 n. 41–42, 100–101 n. 64–65, 101 n. 67, 102 n. 74
Koch Street 95 n. 8

Kraaipan 88 n. 99
Kroonstad 15, 42, 44, 47, 49, 88 n. 103, 89 n. 6, 92 n. 31, 92 n. 36
Kruger, President SJP (Paul, 'Oom Paul') 16, 20, 28, 33 (photo), 34–35, 38, 40– 42, 44, 46, 48–49, 51, 53, 65–66, 70, 83 n. 44, 88 n. 104, 91 n. 21, 92 n. 35, 93 n. 41, 93 n. 47, 99 n. 47

Ladybrand 9, 92 n. 28
Ladysmith 17, 24, 29, 30, 32, 35–36, 80 n. 14, 81 n. 21–22, 84 n. 50–51, 85 n. 62, 85 n. 64, 85 n. 69, 87 n. 85–86
Legislative Assembly (*Volksraad*) last meeting of 48, 92 n. 33
Le Mesurier, Officer 34, 87 n. 82
Lombard's Kop 36, 87 n. 86
Longfellow, HW 42, 90 n. 10
Looting 26, 30, 51–52, 52 (photo), 65, 82 n. 29, 94 n. 53–54
Lourenço Marques 99 n. 47
Louw & Collins 20, 91 n. 27
Lowrie, Miss Frances A 22, 80 n. 6
Lyddite shells, 37, 87 n. 93
Lydenburg 51, 98 n. 35
Lydenburg Commando 11, 88 n. 102

Machadodorp 6, 93 n. 47
Mafeking 17, 24, 28, 49, 82–83 n. 39–40, 85 n. 66, 88 n. 99, 92 n. 35
Magersfontein, Battle of 37, 80 n. 14, 85 n. 66, 87 n. 92
Majuba, Battle of 86 n. 74, 86 n. 80, *See also* Amajuba Day
Malan Mrs 65, 99 n. 49
Malays 40
Malherbe EJB 33, 86 n. 70
Mansvelt, Dr Nicolaas 43, 90 n. 11
Market Street (later Paul Kruger Street) 53 (photo), 95 n. 8
Marks, Samuel (Sammy) 100 n. 56
Marriages between Boer and Brit 68
Martial Law 21, 23, 29, 55, 79 n. 1
Mauser rifles 38, 44, 90 n. 18
Melrose House 6, 18, 74 (photo), 102 n. 75, *See also* Vereeniging, Peace Treaty of
Mental Hospital (*Krankzinnigengesticht*) 53, 94 n. 58
Messum, Dr GB 67, 100 n. 55
Meyer, General LJ (Lucas) 13, 38, 68, 78 n. 23, 87–88 n. 95, 100 n. 57
Meyer, Mrs LJ (Nelly, born Burger) 13, 38, 68, 78 n. 23, 87–88 n. 95, 100 n. 57
Middelberg, GAA 90 n. 12
Middelburg 63
Milner, Sir (later Lord) Alfred 16
Minnaar, JC 27, 82 n. 34
Minnaar Mrs 27
Mobility, Boer 29, 84 n. 52
Modder River 42, 85 n. 66, 86 n. 76, 87 n. 84, 88 n. 98
Modderspruit, Battle of 81 n. 21

INDEX

Morgendaal JJ 73, 101 n. 70
Morning Post 84 n. 58
Murray Mrs Katie 33

Naauwpoort 84 n. 53
National anthem 51
Ncome River, Battle of (Battle of Blood River) 83 n. 41
Nederduitsch Gereformeerde of Hervormde Kerk, See Church, Dutch Reformed
Netherlands-South African Railway Company (NZASM) 90 n. 12
Newspapers, *See De Volksstem* and *The Pretoria Friend*
Neutrality, oath of, 58, 96 n. 17–18, 101 n. 67
Nicholson's Nek, encounter at 81 n. 21
Numerical superiority of British 31, 40, 48–49, 63, 84 n. 60
Nursing staff, Bourke Hospital 22

Oath of neutrality, *See* Neutrality, oath of
Officials, departure of, *See* Government officials leave Pretoria
Opperman Mr 34, 86 n. 81
Opperman, Commandant D (Rooi Daniel) 85 n. 69
Orange Free State 7, 9–10, 15, 36, 40, 42, 47–50, 55–56, 80 n. 17, 86 n. 76,
    88 n. 98, 88 n. 103, 89 n. 5–7, 91 n. 20, 92 n. 28, 92 n. 31, 92 n. 36, 93 n. 41,
    101 n. 69
Orange (Gariep) River 9, 89 n. 7
Orange River Sovereignty 9

Paardeberg, Boer surrender at 19, 20, 35 (photo), 36, 85 n. 66, 86 n. 76
Palace of Justice 88 n. 97
Palapye 86 n. 75
Payne Brothers Outfitters 71 (photo), 100 n. 58
Peace 6, 11, 13, 17–19, 27, 31, 55, 57, 66, 68, 71, 74 (photo), 75, 91 n. 23,
    99 n. 41, 100 n. 56, 102 n. 75, *See also* Vereeniging, Peace Treaty of
Peace emissary, death of 73, 101 n. 70
Permits, issue of 55, 58
Plague, *See* Typhoid, outbreak of
Platrand, Battle of 85 n. 64
Pocklington 9
Poor whites 43, 66, 90 n. 14
Poplar Grove, Battle of 88 n. 98
Postal services 43, 56, 58–59, 66, 82 n. 37
Potgieter, PJ 93 n. 46
Potgieter Street 94 n. 59
Pott, Joe 32
Pretoria Commando 36, 82 n. 29–30
The Pretoria Friend 59, 97 n. 21
Pretoria, occupation of 14, 17–19, 43, 48, 51, 53, 53 (photo), 54 (sketch), 82 n. 37,
    85 n. 67, 87 n. 95, 90 n. 15, 92–93 n. 37–38, 94 n. 62, 95 n. 4, 99 n. 41

Pretorius 24, 80 n. 18
Prinsloo, Commandant H (Hendrik) 85 n. 69
Prinsloo Street 11, 87 n. 88
Prinsloo, Adv WRC (Bill) 7, 77 n. 6
Prior, Melton 54 (sketch)
Proclamations, issued by British 71–72, 96 n. 18, 101 n. 65, 102 n. 74

Red Cross 19, 21–22, 47, 57, 79 n. 2, 85 n. 68, 97 n. 23
Reitz, Deneys 82 n. 29
Reitz, FW 93 n. 47
Removal of state funds from Pretoria, *See* State funds removed from Pretoria
Reyneke, GJ 12, 78 n. 22, 88 n. 95, 92 n. 34
Rhodes, CJ 33, 51, 86 n. 78
Rinderpest 90 n. 14
Roberts, Field Marshal Lord FS 14, 17–19, 41, 44, 54 (sketch), 55, 58, 58 (photo), 61, 83 n. 47, 85 n. 61, 85 n. 66, 87 n. 84, 88 n. 103, 91 n. 19, 93 n. 38, 96 n. 14, 97 n. 21, 97 n. 27, 99 n. 41, 99 n. 42, 100 n. 64
Roses in Pretoria 65
Rustenburg 70

Salaries of officials reduced 51
Salaries of officials unpaid 51–52, 94 n. 51–52, 53, 56, *See also* State funds removed from Pretoria
Schoeman, General H 84 n. 53
Schoeman Street 10, 11, 84 n. 57
School, *See* State Model School
Schools, closure of 21, 79 n. 2, 99–100 n. 50
Schutte, CE 22, 80 n.11, 88 n. 97
Schutte, Mrs CE 88 n. 97
Scorched earth policy, effects of 18, 64, 68–70, 72, 74, 99 n. 42, 100 n. 59, 100 n. 64, 101 n. 67
Sewing group, *See* Women's sewing group
Shortages 6, 19–20, 30, 36, 50, 55–57, 61–67, 70
Sieges, Boers', criticism of 84 n. 52
Six Mile Spruit 52, 65
Skinner Street 11, 80 n. 9, 85 n. 68
Smuts, General JC (Jan) 11, 15–16, 18, 53, 91 n. 27, 93 n. 47, 94 n. 51–52, 94 n. 61, 96 n. 20
Spanish flu epidemic 20
Spionkop, Battle of 32–33, 34, 45, 83 n. 47, 85 n. 62, 85 n. 69, 86 n. 72
Sri Lanka, *See* Ceylon
Staatsgymnasium, *See* State Gymnasium
Staatsmodelschool, *See* State Model School
State funds removed from Pretoria 6, 20, 51, 53, 85 n. 67, 94 n. 51–52
State Gymnasium (*Staatsgymnasium*) 86 n. 81
State Model School (*Staatsmodelschool*) 10–11, 21–23, 23 (photo), 30–31, 33, 34,

56, 79 n. 2, 80 n. 9, 84 n. 56, 84 n. 58, 86 n. 75, 87 n. 82–83, 90 n. 13, 95 n. 10, *See also* Hostel (*Eerste Staatstehuis*)
State Model School Hospital 56, 95 n. 10
State Hospital, *See* Volks Hospital
State Museum 86 n. 81
St Bees 9, 12
Steyn, President MT 10, 42, 93 n. 41
St Helena 71, 100 n. 63
Stormberg, Battle of 80 n. 14, 91 n. 19
Sunnyside 53
Surrender, burghers refusal to 6, 11, 65–66, 70, 72, 93 n. 41, *See also* Proclamations by Kitchener
Surrender of Pretoria, 53, 94 n. 60

Tactics, Boer, criticism of 84 n. 52
Theft, 30, 44–45, 84 n. 54
Theron, Captain Danie 96 n. 17
'Tommies' (British soldiers) 41, 89 n. 4, *See also* 'Khakies'
Troops, British, in Pretoria 53, 53 (photo), 55, 57, 63
Tugela River 32, 34, 36, 45, 85 n. 62
Typhoid, outbreak of 56–57, 96 n. 12, 96 n. 14, 100 n. 52

Uitlanders 16
Ultimatum, Boer 36
Union Jack 41, 48, 54 (sketch)

Vaal River 50
Van Alphen, IN 91 n. 25
Van Alphen, Mrs IN 46, 91 n. 25
Van Broekhuizen, Revd HD 58, 96 n. 17
Van der Merwe, JJ (Johannes) 24, 28, 36, 45, 66, 70, 81 n. 19, 99–100 n. 50
Van der Spuy, Melt 98 n. 32
Van der Spuy, Mrs Melt 61, 98 n. 32
Van der Walt Street 10–11, 80 n. 9, 84 n. 56–57, 88 n. 101, 99 n. 43
Van Reenen's Pass 15, 36, 87 n. 87
Vereeniging, Peace Treaty of 6, 13, 18, 74 (photo), 75, 102 n. 75
Victoria, Queen 48, 72, 100 n. 52, 101 n. 68
Visagie Street 99 n. 43
Volks Hospital (State Hospital) 53, 57, 94 n. 59
Volkslied, *See* National anthem
Volksraad, *See* Legislative Assembly
Volksrust 43–44
Voortrekkers 83 n. 41, 89 n. 3
Voss, TG (Thomas) 52, 55–56 (photo), 58–59, 67–68, 83–84 n. 49, 94 n. 56, 95 n. 6–8, 98 n. 32, 98 n. 36

Voss, Mrs TG 29, 52–53, 55–56, 58–59, 62, 65–69, 83–84 n. 49, 94 n. 56, 95 n. 6–8, 96 n. 16, 98 n. 32, 98 n. 36–37
Voss, Cathie 56, 64, 95 n. 7
Voss, Dorothy 59, 62–65, 67–69, 98 n. 37, 99 n. 44
Voss, George 55, 64, 66–67
Voss, Hester 68
Voss, Lena 62
Voss, Vivian 55–56, 62–64, 98 n. 36, 99 n. 44
Vryheid 47, 50, 68

Waterval 35, 39, 87 n. 83
Watson, Lieutenant WWR 94 n. 60
Wellington 55, 68, 97 n. 22
Wepener 92 n. 30
White, Lieutenant General Sir George 24, 29, 81 n. 21–22, 84 n. 51
Winburg 47, 92 n. 31
Witwatersrand 16
Women and children flee Pretoria 49, 93 n. 40
Women and children, suffering of 14, 18–19, 27–28, 36, 39, 45, 50, 68–69, 73–74, 83 n. 40, 91 n. 23, 100 n. 59, 101 n. 67, 102 n. 73
Women, behaviour of towards soldiers 63, 68, 98–99 n. 40
Women, contribution of 19–20, 38, 49, 58, 92–93 n. 37, 99 n. 49
Women's meeting 92–93 n. 37
Women's sewing group 20, 38, 88 n. 97
Wood, Mrs 32
Woodgate, Major General ERP 85 n. 69